HISTORY OF
ANDERSONVILLE PRISON

Ovid L. Futch

University of Florida Press

A University of Florida Press Book

Library of Congress
Catalog Card No. 68-20413

ISBN 0-8130-0591-4

Seventh printing, 1983

Preface

MANY WRITERS have dealt with Andersonville Prison, but few of them have attempted to approach the subject objectively. No one has written a complete account of the prison based on a scholarly sifting of available evidence. The purpose of this study is to determine what happened at Andersonville, to examine the conditions which resulted in high mortality among the prisoners, and to consider the question of responsibility for those conditions.

No attempt has been made to compare Andersonville with other Civil War prisons. I have refrained from speculating on what might have resulted from continuation of a free exchange of prisoners. Rather, my approach has been to regard the cessation of exchanges as an accomplished fact which did not relieve either side of the obligation to provide for captives taken in battle.

I am deeply indebted to Professor Bell I. Wiley, who drew my attention to this topic and whose skillful guidance has been invaluable in the research and writing. Mr. Joseph P. Renald, Chicago, Illinois, generously shared his incomparable knowledge of the early career of Henry Wirz. Especially helpful information and suggestions have been given by Mrs. Violet Moore, librarian, Montezuma Carnegie Library, Montezuma, Georgia; Mr. Lonnie G. Downs, Montezuma; Mrs. Marian Tate, library assistant, Special Collections Division, University of Georgia Library, Athens; and Dr. Horace Montgomery, Professor of History, University of Georgia. The research which has gone into this endeavor was made possible by a grant from the Southern Fellowships Fund.

Grateful acknowledgment is also given to Mrs. Ovid L. Futch for long hours of proofreading and typing, and for encouragement and inspiration.

A slightly revised version of chapter four appeared as "Prison Life at Andersonville," *Civil War History*, VIII (June, 1962), 121–35; and most of chapter five was incorporated in "Andersonville Raiders," *Civil War History*, II (December, 1956), 47–60. I am grateful to *Civil War History* for permission to reprint these chapters.

OVID L. FUTCH

Contents

1

The Power to Impress

GEORGIA STATE HIGHWAY 49 runs in a southwest-northeast direction through the low hills, marshes, and swamps of southwestern Georgia. About eleven miles northeast of Americus a stretch of the road that straightens out in a north-south line serves as a segment of the boundary between Macon and Sumter counties. The Central of Georgia Railroad, on the west side of the highway in Sumter County, runs through the town of Andersonville, population about 280, while across the road in Macon County is situated Andersonville Prison Park.*

Approximately three hundred yards northwest by north from the park, also in Macon County, is Andersonville National Cemetery. A portion of the north-south line between the two counties is about six hundred yards south of the park where Sweet Water Creek flows eastward on its way to confluence with the Flint River.

Mr. C. W. Schaller, superintendent of the cemetery and park, is also responsible for care of a tract of land across the highway in Sumter County, where a camp of the Civilian Conservation Corps was located during the 1930's. Eight laborers work full time at the job of keeping up the two hundred acres in the cemetery, prison park, and the old CCC camp.

---

* This site was in Sumter County in the 1860's, and the Andersonville Prison Post was officially named Camp Sumter. After the Civil War residents of this corner of Sumter complained of their isolation and requested the state legislature to change the county line so as to make them citizens of Macon County. Their request was granted in 1870. See *Acts and Resolutions of the General Assembly of the State of Georgia, Passed in Atlanta, Georgia, at the Session of 1870*, p. 26.

1

The northbound motorist who turns right from Highway 49 through the entrance to Andersonville Prison Park is confronted by several imposing monuments, erected by various northern states in honor of their troops who died in Andersonville Prison during the Civil War. Exact location of the old prison stockade is indicated by stakes set in the earth. They enclose a rectangular space measuring about 750 feet in an east-west direction and 1,540 feet north and south, or about twenty-six and one-half acres. Approximately eighteen feet inside the stockade line is a second rectangle of stakes marking the deadline beyond which prisoners were not permitted to pass. In other words, the area between stockade wall and deadline was a no man's land which prevented prisoners from approaching the wall. About 150 yards from the south end of the old stockade line, a branch of Sweet Water Creek flows from west to east through the prison.

This stream's right bank rises in a gentle slope to the south; the left bank is much steeper and higher. Various kinds of shrubs, vines, briars, and a wide variety of small trees, including sweet bay, red bay, tupelo, tulip, sweet gum, black gum, myrtle, small magnolia, linden, red-flowering maple, and beech grow so densely in the marshy ground near the stream that to approach it is extremely difficult. A bit farther up from the creek's edge are such trees as long-leaf and yellow pine, persimmon, barren scrub, black jack, post and upland willow oak, black walnut, chinquapin, wild plum, maple, wild haw, and whortleberry.

All of these trees except the pines are stunted and puny in appearance. Still farther up the hillside the treeless ground is covered with Bermuda, St. Augustine, and carpet grasses. Some seventy-five yards from the north end of the prison boundary the ground levels off. This crest commands an excellent view of the scene where some thirteen thousand United States prisoners of war died between February 14, 1864, and May 5, 1865.[1]*

The decision of the Confederate government to locate a prisoner-of-war camp in Southwestern Georgia came as a result of several considerations. The concentration of prisoners in Richmond during the first years of the war required the

* Notes begin on page 123.

importation of additional supplies and increased the burden of the Confederacy's overtaxed transportation system. These importations also helped to inflate Richmond prices. Furthermore, as General Lee pointed out in October, 1863, the prisoners would be a military liability in case of attack by the enemy.[2]

Pressing military necessities forced the Richmond government to send every available soldier to the front and weakened the forces responsible for guarding prisoners. The citizenry feared a prison break and clamored for removal of captives held in their midst.[3] It appeared desirable to remove the prisoners to a place more remote from the seat of war, so that they could be more easily guarded, enemy raids would be less likely, and they could be more easily supplied with food.

In November, 1863, Confederate Secretary of War James A. Seddon ordered Captain W. Sidney Winder to Milledgeville, Georgia, to consult with Governor Joseph E. Brown, then to Atlanta to confer with General Howell Cobb, after which he was to select a prison site near Americus or Fort Valley.[4] Winder considered locating the prison at Blue (now Radium) Springs, near Albany, but opposition by property owners there discouraged him.[5] He then inspected the locality of Magnolia Springs, between Americus and Plains, and apparently would have established the prison at that place but for the objection of members of a Primitive Baptist church, who used the springs for baptismal ceremonies.* The spot he eventually chose was in the midst of Georgia's cotton- and corn-growing section, seven miles west of the Flint River, forty-two miles east of the Chattahoochee, and about sixteen hundred feet east of the depot at Anderson Station.

Anderson had a population of less than twenty souls when Captain Winder located the grounds for the proposed prison.[6] It was named for John W. Anderson, superintendent of the Southwestern Railroad (predecessor of the Central of Georgia) at the time of its extension from Oglethorpe to Americus in the early 1850's. The United States Post Office

---

* Spencer, p. 19; personal interview with Dr. Robert C. Pendergrass, January 20, 1959. Dr. Pendergrass of Americus, Georgia, has devoted many years to study of the prison's history and is conversant with numerous legends connected with it.

Department later changed the name to Anderson*ville* to avoid confusion with Anderson, South Carolina.[7] The land on which the Federal prisoners were to be confined was owned by Wesley W. Turner and Benjamin B. Dykes, the latter having purchased several hundred acres on both sides of the railroad in the late 1850's and early 1860's.[8]

In late December, 1863, Captain Richard B. Winder, a cousin of Sid Winder, received orders to proceed to Andersonville and supervise construction of a stockade for confinement of six thousand prisoners and, as quartermaster for the new post, to arrange facilities for the men who would guard them. Dick Winder observed the steepness of the northern bank of the creek and suggested making the stockade larger than his cousin had originally intended. Before construction began, his recommendation that the stockade be built large enough for ten thousand men had been approved.

Dick Winder's superiors promised him that tools, equipment, and labor for building the new prison would be available without stint. But at least some residents of the surrounding countryside were as unhappy over the prospect of a camp in their midst as those of Albany had been, and they so opposed Winder's efforts that he was obliged "to get authority from Richmond to impress the necessary labor and teams."[9]

Of course it must not be supposed that this neighborhood opposition to the erection of the prison meant that people foresaw the immense graveyard and the "intolerable stench" which would emanate from the stockade. By 1864 the Southern people had learned something about the results of having armed men camped in their midst. The reason for objection to the prison is suggested by a Sumter County soldier who wrote home from Virginia, "we . . . ar all very much oppose to it knowing what destruction it is to a countery to send Soldiers to it."[10] What this veteran soldier feared was the damage which Confederate guards would inflict on the community.

Resort to impressment caused considerable delay in Captain Winder's plans, and it was January, 1864, before the work of cutting down the trees and digging a trench for the stockade got under way. Winder acquired the services of an experienced labor foreman, C. C. Sheppard, former plantation superintendent of Dougherty and Lee counties,[11] and impressed teams, Negro slaves, free Negroes, and tools.[12] By late January the woodland along the sluggish stream that was soon to be called Stockade Creek was resounding to the laughter and song of Negro workmen as their axes felled the majestic pines of that virgin forest.

The design of the prison was simple. Tall, straight pines were cut down, trimmed, and topped so as to make logs about twenty feet in length. Negroes with broadaxes then hewed these logs to a thickness of eight to twelve inches, and the hewn timbers, pointed on top, were planted about five feet deep in a trench, making a wall approximately fifteen feet high. The original stockade enclosed only about sixteen and one-half acres.[13]

The workmen erected sentry boxes along the top of the palisades. The floors of these boxes were placed along the outside of the stockade wall about three and one-half feet from the top so that the top of the stockade logs was about even with the sentry's waist when he stood in the box. The sentry posts were about eighty-eight feet apart, covered with wooden roofs, and accessible by ladders. On the west side were two gates, one on each side of the stream. In front of these gates were exterior semicircular stockades, each having its own outside gate so that prisoners could be brought into the semicircular enclosure and halted while the outside gate was closed, before the gate in the main wall was opened. Workers constructed forts at the northeast, southeast, and southwest corners of the prison and on the east side.[14]

In trying to prepare for the reception of prisoners from Richmond, Captain Winder was beset by numerous difficulties. Confederate Quartermaster General Alexander R. Lawton instructed him to buy beef in Florida and southwestern Georgia to feed the captives, but he had no men to drive stock and no means of getting any.[15] Orders from the Quartermaster General's Office stipulated that he should call upon the nearest commissary of subsistence for supplies, and this was Major A. M. Allen in Columbus, fifty miles from Andersonville. Allen's agent in Americus, Uriah B. Harrold, delivered some beef and other supplies to Winder,[16] but on February 3 the Andersonville quartermaster wrote to Allen, "Mr. Harrold

cannot begin to furnish me with one-half of what I shall
need."[17] Corn and meal gave him no concern; the quartermaster department had promised to furnish these. But he was
most eager to learn in what quantities Allen would be able to
supply him with "beef, meat, flour, sugar, molasses, rice, soap,
candles, &c." Winder would take bacon or beef, whichever
Allen could furnish; he would require very little flour, and
sugar only for the hospital. Intending to make candles at
Andersonville, he requested Allen not to remove the tallow
from the beef being sent him. "All beef which has been here-
tofore sent me by Mr. Harrold, he has (so he says) taken
out the tallow by your orders."

Remoteness from centers of manufacturing presented problems in securing cooking utensils, and Winder was compelled
to send to Cartersville, in northwestern Georgia, for hundred-
gallon kettles to be used for boiling meat. Procurement of
corn and meal proved to be more troublesome than he had
anticipated. His agent contracted with various grist mills in
the vicinity to furnish meal, but the corn which the millers
expected to grind was to be turned over to them by receiving
agents of the government, and the assistant quartermasters
in the several districts frequently failed to issue the necessary
orders to their agents. Even after orders were issued, Winder
could never be sure that the supply of corn would be sufficient.
A week before the first prisoners arrived at Andersonville,
he was begging the quartermaster at Albany, "please forward
all the provisions you can." The uncertain transportation system of the Confederacy caused the harassed Andersonville
quartermaster further worry. Articles paid for and shipped
were not always delivered.

As the day drew near for arrival of the first prisoners,
Winder became more desperate in appeals for aid. On February 20 he wrote Commissary P. W. White, "the prisoners
arrive here today. Please make some arrangement at once
about my supply of bacon which will insure me against failure." He added that he had received only "some 10,000
pounds of bacon ordered to me." White's agent in Americus
had only four or five thousand pounds on hand.

On the same day Captain Winder wrote to his kinsman,
Brigadier General John H. Winder, to find out if the gen-

eral could pull some strings for him. General Winder was in command of the Department of Henrico, with headquarters in Richmond. He had used his influence to get his son, Captain W. Sidney Winder, sent to southwestern Georgia to select the prison site and to get Captain Richard B. Winder, his nephew, made quartermaster at Andersonville. Dick Winder had been told "by reliable authority" that the chief purchasing commissary of Florida, Major P. W. White, had agents throughout the Peninsular State who had already bought large numbers of cattle, which had been driven to Quincy in northwestern Florida. Captain Winder desired that Major White be instructed to turn over or sell to him the beeves at Quincy. "It would be of very great assistance to me." He thought he would be able to get the cattle driven from Quincy to Andersonville, but he made the disappointing discovery that it was "absolutely impossible to hire exempts to drive cattle." Speculation was too profitable. "Such as would be willing to perform this service are physically unable."[18]

Since so much has been said and written about the rations fed the Federal prisoners at Andersonville and so many Southern apologists maintain that the prisoners received the same rations as the guards, it is interesting to note that Captain Winder was at least willing to issue substandard food to the Federals. On a trip to Savannah he suggested to Major J. L. Locke, chief purchasing commissary for Georgia, that he "would gladly feed any offal from the slaughterhouses in Albany that could not readily be kept on hand or forwarded to the army to the prisoners at this post, thereby saving that much provision to the government."

But the price of offal was too high. Through a misunderstanding in instructions, Winder's agent, W. M. Pickett, made some purchases, "paying $2 apiece for the luxury of beef tongues for [the prisoners]," and "50 cents per pound for shank meat and pickled hearts." Upon learning of these prices Winder wrote the Albany quartermaster, Captain W. H. Brotherton, that he would either submit Brotherton's prices to the authorities to find out "if such are the established prices of the commissary, or I will hold the shipment which I have received of you subject to your order. . . . Of course I shall not want any more."[19]

Meanwhile attempts to push work on construction of the prison were encountering similar frustrations. Winder became convinced that it would be much faster and cheaper to use planks instead of logs in building barracks and other structures necessary to the prison and post, but instructions required him to use logs. In a letter to General Winder requesting a change in his orders to allow him to choose between logs and planks at his discretion, he revealed yet additional hinderances to his labors. He was threatened with loss of his impressed labor force. The Negroes had to be returned to their homes at the end of sixty days. On February 17 he still had not paid his detailed men for January because instructions from General Winder and Major Locke were in conflict concerning the rate at which he should pay them. He had just learned that the guard being sent to Andersonville was inadequate, and the troops who had already arrived were without guns.

Captain Winder arranged with a citizen of Sumter County to set up a sawmill and grist mill only four miles from Andersonville to saw and grind for the post. The sawmill was also to supply six-by-eight-inch stringers for the railroad, "and the plank which comes off the sides of these will give me the requisite lumber" for the plank structures he desired to build, thus providing for both the railroad and government without injury to either. Promising to use logs where practical, he urged General Winder to grant him permission to use some planks too, "as a portion of the work will await your instruction in this matter."[20]

Major A. M. Allen, who had been appointed Andersonville commissary, wanted Captain Winder to have a house built for him at the post. Winder was more than willing to comply, but could not "get lumber sufficient to do my own work." He informed Allen that Allen must furnish his own materials, for which Winder was willing to pay, "but not at the price of $100 per thousand, which was the price that Captain Armstrong [Allen's assistant] informed me he could purchase lumber at." If Allen had authority to impress lumber, "come at once and impress the necessary mills, or give me the power, and we can in this way get the lumber."

Two weeks later Winder wrote to assure Allen that "I

will do anything that I can to facilitate you in your department at this post" and that he was at work on the major's house. But lack of lumber and materials would retard him. Winder himself was using the church until his own house could be completed, which would be soon. He promised to let Allen have the church "certainly by next Monday week." But it was imperative that Allen render assistance in obtaining materials. Could he buy nails, door fastenings, and window glass in Columbus? Winder had "applied to the Secretary of War for authority to impress mills." Granting this request would remove all obstacles to completion of Allen's house.[21]

Captain Winder's labor force was adequate, and his great desire for power to impress lumber was finally gratified. But contrary to his assumption, he found that other impediments to his work remained. He was unable to get the lumber transported, and tools and nails were impossible to obtain. The troops were suffering from lack of tents, which were unavailable. Part of his burden was removed by an order of the Richmond government making the commissary department responsible for feeding prisoners of war. Consequently Winder could stop worrying about horses to drive cattle from Florida, but he still needed wagons, harness, bridles, an ambulance, and either mules or horses to transport hospital stores and meet the requirements of the quartermaster department at Andersonville.[22]

These difficulties experienced by the architects and builders of Andersonville Prison are suggestive of the troubles that continued to beset its administrators throughout its existence. There is something pathetic about Dick Winder's futile entreaties for supplies and equipment for Andersonville. One gets the impression from reading his letters that a man more capable of efficient organization and more skilled in handling men might have achieved greater success. But it can never be known to what extent his failure was due to his ineptitude or to what extent it was an unavoidable result of the dwindling fortunes of the Confederacy. The prisoners of war who were to suffer and die in Andersonville during the approaching months would reap a portion of the results of a government's attempt to do more than it was capable of doing.

In the midst of preparations to receive the Federal captives, with the stockade only about half-completed, Commandant of the Post Captain W. Sidney Winder received notice that it was no longer possible to feed the prisoners at Richmond and that they must be sent to Andersonville at once.[23] The first batch of prisoners, five hundred from Belle Isle, left Richmond on February 18 and arrived at Andersonville on Thursday, February 25, 1864.[24] Entering the unfinished stockade, they found themselves facing Confederate artillery where palisades had not yet been erected.[25]

2

Gross Mismanagement

THE DIFFICULTY which Captain Richard B. Winder encountered in his attempts to obtain lumber prevented construction of barracks for the prisoners. His proposal to impress sawmills brought a storm of protests from railroad owners who insisted that it would lead to the complete breakdown of transportation. The government then ordered Winder to impress no mills which sawed for the railroads. As a result, most mill-owners signed contracts to furnish small quantities to some railroad and disposed of the remainder of their output as they pleased. They would not sell to Winder because he had orders to pay no more than fifty dollars per thousand board feet, "while the navy works at Albany and the hospital departments were paying $75 or $80 per 1,000."[1]

Realizing the impossibility of building barracks under these circumstances, Winder requested tents for the prisoners. He argued that tents would be more healthful than frame houses, less expensive, and less of a fire hazard. But the quartermaster general informed him that tents "could not be supplied for the simple reason they did not have them." Winder attempted to get some tents from the state of Georgia, stored at Savannah, but was told they were required for the use of Confederate troops.

Many writers have attempted to show that the Confederacy deliberately sought to bring about the death of Federal prisoners of war at Andersonville. One of the proofs frequently adduced to sustain this accusation was the failure of prison authorities to provide shelter for the prisoners though forests of virgin timber lay on every side.[2] But the records

11

reveal a sincere but unsuccessful effort to provide housing for the prisoners.

Another continuing difficulty was inadequate transportation. Captain Winder obtained authority from Major Norman W. Smith, chief inspector of field transportation for the First Military District, to impress wagons and teams, and then he called on Sheriff W. B. Paul of Lee County to take four teams of four mules each from the plantations best able to spare them for thirty days.[3] Of course such paltry measures were unequal to the deficiencies at Andersonville. Winder received information that a trainload of lumber had been awaiting transportation at Gordon for twelve days. He wrote Major J. G. Michaeloffsky, quartermaster at Macon, begging him to take "the most decided and prompt action" to have it shipped to Andersonville to meet "the very great emergency" existing there. "I am burying the dead without coffins. . . . If [the lumber] is not here in a reasonable period I shall be compelled to report the matter to the authorities at Richmond."[4]

It is fairly obvious that part of the suffering and death at Andersonville was attributable to the paucity of developed southern resources. What may be less obvious, though no less important, is that some of it came as a result of short-sighted management and lack of administrative ability. On February 7, while the prison was under construction, Confederate Adjutant and Inspector General Samuel Cooper asked Brigadier General Howell Cobb, commander of the Georgia State Guard which had expired three days previously, to recommend an efficient commandant for Camp Sumter, Confederate States Military Prison at Andersonville.[5] Cooper thought the commandant should be a Georgian, a colonel or a brigadier general, unassigned because of wounds or some other disability. Colonel Magill of the First Georgia Infantry had sought the appointment, but Cooper feared "he will not answer, and I understand further that his record is not altogether such as would entitle him to so responsible a command."[6]

Lieutenant Colonel Alexander W. Persons of the Fifty-fifth Georgia, formerly of Fort Valley, was ordered to Andersonville on February 26 to command the prison guard and take charge of the prisoners. Three days later he replaced Sid

Winder as commandant of the post, which position he held until relieved in early June.[7] Persons' relations with superior and inferior officers seem to have been cordial enough, and he was apparently well liked by the prisoners.[8] One of the most bitter of anti-Southern writers concedes that "as far as his knowledge and experience of the requirements of his position permitted, he expended all the facilities in his power to mitigate the condition in which his prisoners were placed."[9]

Sid Winder had reported regularly to his father, General John H. Winder, who was in charge of war prisons in the vicinity of Richmond. The general was annoyed by the appointment of Persons without instructions to report to him. He asked Secretary of War Seddon for a definition of his connection with Andersonville. "It would be embarrassing for me to issue orders when I had no right to do so, and it would be just as embarrassing for me to neglect to issue orders when I ought to do so." Seddon forwarded Winder's communication to Adjutant General Cooper, who replied that he saw no difficulty in the case. General Winder, as a veteran officer, must know that the commander of a military post, whether or not it held prisoners, was "the commander of everything that appertains to that post." If Winder lacked confidence in Persons, let him name a successor who would satisfy him. Winder answered that he had been misunderstood, protesting that he had no desire to raise a question, but that Persons' orders assigned him to command at Andersonville without saying to whom he should report.[10] This is typical of the trivia which commanded the attentions and absorbed the energies of those responsible for the administration of Andersonville Prison.

Special Order Number 75, issued March 30, 1864, assigned Brigadier General Howell Cobb to command of the newly authorized Reserve Corps of Georgia.[11] Less than two weeks after Cobb established his headquarters at Macon, he was receiving requests from Andersonville for troops, artillery, and ammunition. He replied that ammunition was on its way, that he had no artillery, and that troops for guard duty would be sent as soon as his command was organized, unless he received contrary orders.[12]

Not until April 27 was Cobb ordered to supply the guard for Andersonville, but he took an active interest in the prison from the time he set up his headquarters in Macon. He wrote Adjutant General Cooper on April 18: "Col. O'Neal is here from Andersonville. He can give you much valuable information about the camp. I would suggest that he be ordered to Richmond with that view." Next day he expressed to Brigadier General Hugh Weeden Mercer, commander of the Georgia brigade at Savannah, the opinion that with the guard then at Andersonville, it was "not safe." A few days later he advised Mercer against removing the Fifty-seventh Georgia from Andersonville. Such action Cobb believed would be "attended with serious danger of the prisoners escaping."[13]

In addition to the Fifty-seventh Georgia, guard units at Andersonville included the Fifty-fifth and Fifty-sixth Georgia regiments and the Twenty-sixth Alabama. Those regular troops were of course needed at the front. Prisoners were arriving faster than preparations could be made to receive them, workmen labored daily to improve the security of the prison, and the prison keepers worried constantly for fear their charges would escape. The plea for Cobb to send troops to Andersonville was the more urgent because the regulars might be ordered away at any time.

Cobb promised to "send the first regiment organized to Andersonville."[14] But organization was seriously impeded by the policies of Governor Brown, who, according to one newspaper, was "too tenacious of state and county officials."[15] Cobb engaged in a lengthy controversy with the governor, his political enemy, urging upon Brown the great need for men and complaining of the "sweeping exemption of all civil and military officers of the state." In his correspondence with Adjutant General Cooper, Cobb blamed Brown for the fact that the Reserve Corps would be smaller than anticipated.[16]

Meanwhile Colonel Persons was trying to get lumber for prison barracks and other buildings needed at Andersonville. Relating his difficulties later he said, "The railroad upon which the prison was located was worked to its greatest capacity in feeding Lee's and Johnston's armies, and it was with the greatest difficulty that I could get transportation. . . . Perhaps in ten or twenty days they would give me one train. I held constant communication with the superintendent of the road, and every time I could get a train, I would have that train loaded with lumber and brought through. During my stay, I had concentrated there, I suppose, about five or six train-loads of lumber. I suppose there were six or eight or ten cars in a train. There were altogether about fifty carloads. I was in the act of erecting shelter, was just carrying the lumber, when I was relieved. . . . I went into the stockade several times after I was relieved from duty, and I saw no shelter there. I saw forty or fifty houses springing up outside of the grounds. The lumber disappeared in that way."[17]

Lack of tools also was a great handicap. Soon after Persons' arrival at Andersonville, eight thousand prisoners were in the stockade and "not an axe, hoe, spade, shovel, &c., could be had." Absence of police and sanitary regulations in the prison soon produced a filthy condition which resulted in much sickness and disease and a frightful rate of mortality. Warned by his medical board that the prison must be thoroughly renovated, Persons "wrote throughout the State and tried by proxy to supply the prison" with necessary tools, but his efforts were of no avail. Lacking even the tools needed for burying the dead, he learned "that I could be supplied with the things I so much needed in Augusta." His regimental quartermasters were away from the post looking for hospital tents and clothing for troops. Quartermaster Dick Winder was "in bed sick with inflammatory rheumatism." Under these circumstances Persons himself went to Augusta. His absence from Andersonville was discovered by Adjutant General Cooper, who telegraphed him for an explanation. Persons claimed that his "mission was successful and the recent condition of the encampment with its improved health and the contagious diseases in abatement are witnesses in my favor."[18]

Nevertheless Cooper soon afterward asked General Cobb to recommend some brigadier general as a replacement for Persons. Cobb suggested Brigadier General S. R. Anderson of Tennessee. He warned Cooper that security of the prison at Andersonville required "the presence of an officer of rank and efficiency." The number of prisoners was increasing daily "and the guard [remained] comparatively small. It will be increased with men who have never seen service—and strict discipline by efficient officers will be demanded."[19]

Colonel Persons had already given charge of the prisoners

to Captain Henry Wirz.[20] General Lew Wallace, president of the military commission which sent Wirz to the gallows for conspiring to destroy Federal prisoners of war at Andersonville, described him as follows: "He had a small head; retreating forehead, high on the os *frontis* because the hair, light in colour, is very thin, threatening him with speedy baldness; prominent ears; small, sharp pointed mustache and beard heavy enough to conceal the mouth and lower face, and of the dirty-tobacco-stained colour; eyes large, and of mixed blue and grey."[21]

Heinrich Hartmann Wirz, son of a tailor named Hans Caspar Wirz, was born November 25, 1823 (not 1822 as many have written), at 26 Froschaugasse, Zurich, Switzerland. He attended elementary school and the lower Gymnasium, began his commercial training at the Kaufhaus in Zurich, and completed it in Turin, Italy, in 1842. His interests lay in the direction of medical study, but his father objected and insisted on his entering the mercantile field. From 1843 to 1846 he worked with his father. In 1845 he married Emilie Oschwald who bore him two children, Emilie (1847) and Paul (1849). At some time between 1846 and 1849 he ran into trouble with the law. Just what his offense was "is not clear but it had to do with money." Perhaps it was embezzlement; perhaps he lived beyond his means and incurred a debtor's sentence. At any rate he served a brief prison term, his marriage ended in divorce, and apparently the Swiss government banished him. He sailed to America in 1849.*

Wirz worked for a while as a weaver in a factory in Lawrence, Massachusetts, then wandered. In early 1854 he went

---

* For information on Wirz's early career the writer is indebted to Mr. Joseph P. Renald. Mr. Renald has been gathering information on Wirz's life for several years and has had access to family records in Europe. He explodes the fiction that Wirz was a trained physician. Although Wirz wrote General James H. Wilson on May 7, 1865, "I am . . . by profession a physician" *(Wirz Trial,* p. 17), he could not have had a degree from any European university; and Mr. Renald has found "absolutely no evidence that he ever obtained an M.D. degree." He was a bath attendant at a time when medical men thought highly of balneotherapeutics, and it is possible that a New England diploma mill awarded him a certificate for completing some six-month "medical" course; but the Confederacy would hardly have failed to assign him to the sadly overburdened medical service if he had possessed any sort of medical credentials.

to Hopkinsville, Kentucky, and became assistant to a Doctor Weber. He left Weber after two months and went to work for Dr. Edward Caspari, who practiced medicine in Louisville and Brownsboro, Kentucky. Shortly he moved to Cadiz, Kentucky, to set up in practice for himself, and there on May 28, 1854, he married a widow named Elizabeth Wolfe. If Wirz attempted to pose as a physician in Cadiz, he evidently failed to deceive the local doctors. He left Kentucky and drifted to the Marshall plantation at Milliken's Bend, Louisiana, where he was staying—possibly employed as the "doctor" for Mr. Marshall's slaves—when he decided to join the Confederate army.

Enlisting in the Fourth Louisiana Infantry on June 16, 1861, Wirz became a sergeant before he suffered an incurable wound just above the right wrist in the Battle of Seven Pines (May 31, June 1, 1862). This injury was a source of physical suffering right up to the moment the noose tightened about his neck. Promoted to the rank of captain on June 12, 1862, Wirz was detailed shortly afterward as acting adjutant general to General John H. Winder, who assigned him to command the military prison at Richmond in late August. A month later he was sent to search for missing records in Alabama and was subsequently given command of the prison at Tuscaloosa. On December 19, 1862, he received a furlough to go as special plenipotentiary of President Davis on a mission to Paris and Berlin. After remaining in Europe for over a year, Wirz returned to the Confederacy in February, 1864, and on March 27, 1864, was ordered to Andersonville, where Persons assigned him to command of the interior of the prison.[22]

On April 1 the stockade designed for 10,000 men held 7,160 prisoners. Between that date and the eighth of May, 5,787 men arrived from various places, 728 died, 13 escaped, and 7 were recaptured, making a total of 12, 213 inmates on May 8.[23] As the large number of deaths indicates, the condition of the prison had become very unhealthful. Dick Winder, in selecting a site for the prison bakery and cookhouse, had, as he later admitted, committed a grievous error in judgment. Aware that these establishments would require much water, Winder ordered their construction on the creek flowing through the prison, a short distance upstream from the stockade. He said that he supposed the refuse from them would be too small in quantity to pollute the stream, in which supposition he was tragically mistaken.

A second cause of high mortality during the early weeks of the prison's existence was, according to Chief Surgeon Isaiah H. White, "the debilitated condition in which many of the prisoners were when admitted into the prison, having been confined for a long time in other prisons." In addition "small-pox was introduced into the prison by prisoners sent from Richmond." But lack of facilities at Andersonville prevented effective treatment of the sick. Surgeon White reported that on April 25, of 2,697 patients treated, 718 had died, and he pointed to "the absence of proper hospital accommodation" as one explanation for the large ratio of deaths.[24] The hospital for prisoners was located inside the stockade, and drainage from the prison sinks passed through the hospital grounds. Prisoners who were well stole food, hospital bedding, and other supplies from their sick comrades. To protect hospital patients from pilferers and to prevent the continued spread of disease among the prisoners, White urged removal of the hospital outside the stockade.

The first prisoners, finding themselves shelterless, constructed huts and lean-tos from the logs, limbs, bushes, shrubs, and brush left within the prison. They also used whatever materials they brought with them, such as blankets, tent flies, and overcoats. But unfortunately their captors had not completed preparations for receiving them, and no one gave any direction to their efforts. The prisoners followed personal whims in locating and building their huts. This failure on the part of prison authorities to lay off streets and have the prisoners construct their quarters in rows was a tragic omission. It resulted in a hodgepodge of structures that rendered policing of the prison practically impossible after it became crowded. Despite the fact that the post was undermanned, it seems surprising that no one had the foresight or took the time to systematize the arrangement of prison dwellings. Even a rough plan would have made future work much easier and would have saved many lives.

Another source of sickness and disease was the prison fare. Arrangements for cooking and baking were unfinished when prisoners began arriving; the first prisoners received uncooked rations. At that time ample wood was available in the stockade, but many prisoners lacked cooking utensils, and their guardians could furnish none. The bakery and cookhouse were not completed until May, and even then the bread was of inferior quality. Wirz reported that the bread issue consisted "fully of one-sixth of husk, that it is almost unfit for use and [is] increasing dysentery and other bowel complaints. . . . If the meal, such as it is now, was sifted the bread rations would fall short fully one-quarter of a pound."[25] He could not issue beans, molasses, rice, or vinegar because of a shortage of buckets.

When the first prisoners arrived, no arrangements had been made for sewage disposal. It was intended that they should use the lower end of the stream for elimination of wastes, but orders to do so were not enforced and the prison was soon reeking with the filth of thousands of men. After Wirz arrived, he planned to build two dams across the stream and have the prisoners use the water above the first dam for drinking and that between dams for bathing, while latrines, or "sinks," as they were called by Civil War participants, were to be constructed below the second dam. By opening the flood gates of the two dams once a day, the filth of the sinks below could be flushed away. Lack of tools delayed the beginning of this project until May, and it was never completed.

As more and more prisoners arrived, lack of space became an increasingly serious problem. The amount of space per man was reduced by erection of the deadline, marked by scantlings nailed on top of poles driven in the ground eighteen feet inside the stockade wall. The deadline was put up in order to reduce the danger of escapes by keeping prisoners away from the wall and to prevent trading between guards and prisoners.

The condition of prisoners upon arrival at Andersonville, introduction of contagious diseases into the camp, pollution of the stream by waste from the cookhouse and bakery, location of the prisoners' hospital within the stockade, inadequate hospital accommodations, disorderly arrangement of prisoners' quarters, exposure to the elements, absence of police and sanitary regulations, short and defective rations, and overcrowding—all of these contributed to the ever mounting rate of mortality. Reports of prison officials and inspecting officers urged the erection of hospital buildings outside the prison, and when General Cobb visited Andersonville in early May, he recommended to the Richmond government that no more prisoners be sent there until the stockade could be enlarged.[26]

The condition of the prison at this time was described in some detail by Captain Walter Bowie of the Fortieth Virginia, who was ordered by the adjutant and inspector general to make a thorough and minute inspection and report his findings to Richmond.[27] Up to the ninth of May 13,218 prisoners had been received at Andersonville. Of these, 1,026 had died. Bowie found the ground bordering both sides of Stockade Creek, about one-fourth of the total area within the stockade, "altogether unfit for an encampment." He estimated that the prisoners had only about forty-two square feet of space per man. He stated that Captain Wirz hoped to get rid of this swamp by digging drainage ditches and would have done so already but for lack of tools. Bowie suggested that if barracks could not be built, it would be necessary to furnish tents for the prisoners with the coming of summer. The prison, he thought, should be "divided off into proper streets, admitting a free circulation of air and affording better facilities for enforcement of the necessary police regulations."

Guard strength on May 9, according to Bowie, was 1,193. On duty each day were 303 infantrymen and two artillery sections of two guns each. One man occupied each sentry box, forty men were posted outside each gate during the day— eighty at night—and the remainder formed a line around the stockade fifty yards from it. The artillery was stationed so as to command the gates and interior of the prison. At this time no one doubted that the prison was secure, but prison officials were fearful of the result if the guard should be changed, as contemplated, by the substitution of reserves for the regular troops then at Andersonville. The reserves, Bowie reported, were raw recruits, chiefly boys too young or men too old for regular service. They were "entirely unaccustomed to guard duty and liable to the numerous diseases that are incident to the commencement of camp life."

Bowie found that the commissary department was well supplied with provisions, that the cooking and baking facilities had just been completed, and that it was now possible to issue cooked rations to all prisoners on hand. Rations were "the same as those issued to Confederate soldiers in the field, viz., one pound of beef, or in lieu thereof one-third pound of bacon and one quarter pound meal." On occasion rice, beans or peas, molasses, and vinegar were issued. For purposes of issuing rations, taking the roll, and maintaining discipline, the prisoners were divided into detachments of 270 men each, with each detachment being subdivided into three equal squads. Each squad of 90 was further subdivided into three messes of 30 men. Each squad had a sergeant whose duty it was to see that each mess in his squad received its proper portion of the ration, and a sergeant of each mess was responsible for equable distribution of rations in his mess. These sergeants received a double ration for their services.

Each detachment also had a sergeant whose duty it was to see that his 270 men fell into ranks in their proper place promptly at seven o'clock each morning. In case of an absence the sergeant was to report the name of the missing man "and the cause of his absence immediately to the commander of the prison, a failure to do which is severely punished." Sergeants of detachments were also required to escort the sick to the hospital after roll call, and to return to their quarters those sick prisoners not admitted to the hospital. Prisoners in the hospital and those paroled to work outside as cooks, bakers, clerks, and so on were accounted for in the roll books, and as soon as they were discharged from the hospital or had completed their work, they returned to their detachments. Absence from roll call was punished by loss of a day's ration. Those prisoners guilty of minor infractions of prison regulations were forced to work, the rule limiting this enforced labor to a maximum of two hours. Prisoners were forbidden to trade with anyone other than the prison sutler appointed by the post commander.

Bowie reported that no visitors were permitted inside the stockade without a pass from the commandant of the post or the approval and escort of the officer of the day. Authorized visitors were not permitted to converse with prisoners except in the presence of the officer of the day. Wagons entering the stockade to carry commissary goods, hospital supplies, or sutler's stores were examined by the officer of the day to assure that they contained no articles of contraband. Any prisoner who escaped and was recaptured was "punished by having attached to him a ball and chain" for the remainder of his confinement.

When wood in the stockade first began to get scarce, prisoners were permitted to go outside occasionally with a guard to collect wood for fuel and shelter. But shortly before Captain Bowie's inspection, Wirz had found it necessary to withdraw this privilege "owing to too great an intimacy which sprung up between the prisoners and their guard, the exchanging of clothing, &c." Prisoners were allowed to correspond with friends and relatives and a letter box was placed inside the stockade for deposit of mail. Letters were closely censored.[28] Contents of boxes sent to prisoners from friends were carefully examined, after which they were delivered to the addressees. Boxes bearing names of deceased prisoners were turned over to the chief surgeon for hospital use. Prisoners' money was turned over to the quartermaster and the prisoners were allowed to draw on it only for purchase of articles which the sutler was licensed to sell.

Bowie also noted that an attempt had been made to provide for policing the prison. Two squads of twenty-five prisoners each were detailed every day, supplied with shovels, and ordered to remove all waste and filth from the stockade. They burned what was combustible and threw the remainder "into the ditch through which the stream of water flows." Each squad had a superintendent whose duty was to report to Captain Wirz any infraction of police regulations or failure of a detailed man to perform his work satisfactorily.

The inspecting officer rated the hospital as "extremely indifferent." The sick were without shelter except for thirty-five badly worn tent flies. The hospital was still inside the stockade and it had become terribly overcrowded, patients being "crowded in almost as thick as they can be placed." From the establishment of the prison to May 9 some 4,588 patients received treatment, 1,026 died, and 582 were still in the hospital. In addition, according to information given to Bowie by Surgeon White, "nearly 500 . . . [are] under treatment who are not in hospital because there are no accommodations for them." There had been "a considerable increase in the mortality during the past week," and Bowie believed the increase would continue if nothing were done to improve hospital facilities and care of the sick. "At the earnest request of the officers commanding the prison and the surgeon in chief," he suggested that permission be granted for removal of the hospital outside the stockade and that enough tents be supplied for one thousand patients.

The clothing and persons of prisoners were described as "extremely dirty." Bowie questioned prisoners about this condition, and they told him their supply of soap was very small. Wirz admitted the truth of the prisoners' statement and said that the commissary had been unable to obtain an adequate supply. Bowie seemed to think that Doctor White and Captain Wirz were blameless in the condition of affairs at Andersonville. He accepted as a matter of course the fact that when the guards and prisoners became too intimate on wood detail, the remedy was to punish the prisoners by discontinuing the wood-gathering rather than by improving discipline among the troops. Between April 25 and May 9 the surgeons and their aides treated 1,891 prisoners, 308 of whom died. Captain Bowie noted the rising mortality and predicted that it would increase under existing conditions, but observed that "the surgeon in charge . . . seems to attend faithfully to his duties, and regrets exceedingly that he has been furnished with no better hospital accommodations." In truth the scanty facilities were not Doctor White's fault, nor was Wirz to blame for the lack of tools and supplies in the stockade. Bowie was happy to testify "to the ability and efficiency of Captain Wirz, the commander of the prison. His activity and zeal in the discharge of his arduous duties is highly commendable."

In late April General Cobb received orders from Richmond to supply Andersonville with whatever guard he thought necessary for security of the prisoners there.[29] On May 3 General Braxton Bragg telegraphed Cobb that he must send two regiments to Andersonville. On the ninth Cobb wrote Colonel Persons that they would arrive in a few days. He said that orders from Richmond were to relieve Colonel O'Neal's regiment (Twenty-sixth Alabama) first, and Cobb suggested the other regulars at Andersonville be retained until the reserves could be drilled and taught their duties.[30] One week later the Secretary of War ordered the Forty-seventh, Fifty-fifth, and Fifty-sixth Georgia, and the Twenty-sixth Alabama regiments to proceed immediately by railroad to Richmond.[31] This left the guard situation at Andersonville in a dubious state. Cobb forwarded a batch of prisoners from Macon on the twentieth and wrote Persons to keep "the company of the 3d Regt [reserves] that accompanies the prisoners today until further orders if you deem it necessary. You can make a detail from them to return for their camp equipage &c. if necessary." He decided upon this action without consulting the Macon post commandant, Colonel D. Wyatt Aiken, but simply informed him of the pressure "for additional guard at Andersonville," and ordered him to direct the company to remain there.[32]

Three days later Cobb expressed to General H. R. Jackson, commanding at Savannah, his concern over sources of troops if needed in an emergency "to aid in the guarding of these prisoners which is now becoming a serious question." The same day he sent two more companies of the Third Georgia Reserves and promised Persons that he would continue to reinforce the Andersonville guard to the limit of his power.[33] One hundred and fifty more men of the same regiment followed the next day, and Cobb promised to send the remainder of the regiment two days later. He inquired if Persons would still need men, and if so, how many.[34] The Confederate military establishment had by this time become worried for the safety of Atlanta, and Cobb and Persons faced the danger of being left short of troops to act as prison guards by a call to defend that city.

Andersonville was not under Cobb's command, but it was his duty to supply the guard and he was anxious to make it as secure as possible. He wrote to Major Timothy M. Furlow in Americus on May 26 that he had "not regarded the guard as entirely sufficient since the withdrawal of the old troops," which action was taken by his superiors. But Cobb had been doing his best to increase the guard, and, promising to send another regiment down on May 28, he expressed his belief that these troops "with the force already there properly managed ought to make the Prison entirely secure." Still he would endeavor to send more men if they were required.

One great need in late May was enlargement of the prison. This not only would be a boon to the terribly overcrowded prisoners but, as General Cobb believed, would make the prison secure. For the labor Negroes were needed, and Cobb felt that "it is far better for those of us who have negroes to send them promptly and voluntarily and have this work done than to hazard on the escape of the prisoners." Cobb declared himself "more than willing" to send his share. If other interested persons would do likewise, he added, all reason for anxiety would be dispelled in a few days.[35]

Major Thomas P. Turner, after an inspection trip to Andersonville, reported to Richmond on May 25 that he had found parts of the camp extremely filthy, owing to neglect of drainage and policing of the grounds.[36] He reported much difficulty arising from confusion "in regard to rank among the officers, quarrels and contentions as to who ranks and commands, all tending to disturb the good order, discipline and proper conduct of the post and prison." Turner suggested that the post commandant should have sufficient rank and experience to silence all quarrels if he were to have control over the prison. If not, the commandant of the prison should be made independent of the post commandant, and should have the rank necessary for controlling those who reported to him for duty each day. Major Turner felt called upon "to add a word in relation to the officer commanding the interior prison (the prison proper) Captain Wirz, who in my opinion, deserves great credit for the good sense and energy he has displayed in the management of the prison at Andersonville. He is the only man who seems to fully comprehend his important duties. He does the work of commandant, adjutant, clerk, and warden, and without his presence at Camp Sumter at this time, everything would be chaos and confusion; in my opinion, at least two commissioned officers should be assigned to duty to assist him."

In the "gross mismanagement and want of system" which this inspecting officer found at Andersonville lies a part of the explanation for high mortality among the prisoners there, and perhaps his comments on Wirz provide a clue to how a military commission was able to place on him the onus of the Andersonville tragedy. In doing "the work of commandant, adjutant, clerk, and warden," the pain-racked prison-keeper was placed in a position to be blamed for the imperfections of that work. Turner, "judging from the energy which has marked Captain Wirz's conduct in respect to the management of the prisoners at Andersonville," believed that improvements would continue. But no government operating on the scanty resources of the Confederacy in 1864 could afford the luxury of such bickering as was prevalent in management of Confederate prisons in general and in the management of Andersonville in particular.

Insofar as location of the hospital was concerned, Major Turner considered it "the very worst place possible for it," and expressed the view that "any sensible man who has any experience in the management of prisons will, upon inspection of this post agree with me."* Finding Stockade Creek too small and sluggish for the needs of such a large number of prisoners, he recommended the digging of wells on the higher ground. No Federal officers were to be held at Andersonville, but if it were to be made the grand rendezvous point for enlisted men captured throughout the Confederacy, as orders from Richmond indicated, Turner deemed it imperative that another stockade be built similar to the one already being used.[37] He recommended that the new stockade be erected on Sweet Water Creek about one-quarter of a mile south of the existing camp, where flowed a stream "of a volume and velocity at least ten times greater than the one which runs through the grounds now occupied." Barracks should be erected for winter and tents furnished for prisoners in the meantime, he added; otherwise "they will die off by hundreds, and will be a dead loss to us in the way of exchange."

Major Turner was concerned about the guard problem. The reserves from General Cobb's command who had replaced regular troops on guard at Andersonville were for the most part officered by reliable men who had seen service. But a recent War Department order to conscript and send these

---

* Howell Cobb, after inspecting Andersonville three weeks earlier, reported that construction of hospital buildings outside the stockade was the most pressing need, and added, "Upon that point there cannot be two opinions among intelligent men" (O.R., Ser. 2, VII, 120).

officers to the field would leave the Reserve Corps almost completely disorganized. New officers would have to be elected, "and there is scarcely one man out of a hundred who knows the manual of arms or who is capable of marching a company a square." Enforcement of this order would endanger security of the prison. The Florida line was only a little over one hundred miles from Andersonville and Federal forces not much farther, and Turner thought it quite possible that by preconcerted arrangements between these troops and the prisoners, an outbreak might be executed which two or three thousand undisciplined, disorganized, raw recruits without experienced officers would be powerless to stop.

In conclusion, Major Turner expressed the opinion that the Confederacy needed a chief administrator for all its prisons, to prescribe general and comprehensive rules and regulations, establish order and system, and enforce strict discipline. This recommendation was not adopted, but on June 3 President Davis ordered to Andersonville, as the best qualified available officer to command that post, General John H. Winder.[38]

John Henry Winder, sixty-four years of age in 1864, was the son of William H. Winder, that luckless general of the War of 1812 who commanded the militia which fled before the British troops at the Battle of Bladensburg, permitting the enemy to burn and plunder Washington. Long-time residents of Maryland, the Winders were descended from John Winder of Cumberland, England, who came to America around 1665.[39] Grandnephew of Levin Winder, anti-war governor of Maryland during the War of 1812, John Henry was born February 21, 1800, at Rewston, Somerset County, Maryland. He graduated from the United States Military Academy at West Point in 1820, entered the artillery service, and became an instructor of tactics at the Academy. Though he held this position part of the time that Jefferson Davis was a cadet, the latter had no particular knowledge of him as a teacher.[40] Winder resigned in 1823, returned to service in 1827, served with distinction in the Seminole Indian War, and in the Mexican War "was with Genl. Scott from Vera Cruz to the City of Mexico." He participated in the fighting at La Hoya Pass and Chapultepec and was brevetted major for gallantry at Contreras and Cherubusco. For gallantry in the battles before Mexico City he was brevetted lieutenant colonel; he later served as lieutenant governor of Veracruz.[41]

Winder, having spent most of his army years in the South, chose to cast his lot with that section when the Civil War came. Aroused against the Lincoln government by the Baltimore riot of April 19, 1861,[42] Winder mailed his letter of resignation from the army the following day, and ten days later Colonel Lorenzo Thomas wrote him that his resignation had been accepted.[43] On May 18 he became colonel of the First Regiment of Infantry in the State Troops of North Carolina, but a month later the "stout gray-haired old man" was in Richmond seeking a commission as a brigadier general, which he obtained June 21, 1861.[44] Clerk J. B. Jones in the Confederate War Department observed that the applicant was the son of General William H. Winder "whose command in the last war with England unfortunately permitted the City of Washington to fall into the hands of the enemy." This clerk had "almost a superstitious faith in *lucky* generals, and a corresponding prejudice against unlucky ones, and their progeny."[45]

These words, written with reference to one whose name was destined to become linked permanently with the horrors of Andersonville Prison, were ominous ones. Jones could not "suppose the President will order this general into the field. He may take the prisoners into his custody—and do other jobs as a sort of head of military police." Davis appointed Winder provost marshal and commander of Federal prisons in Richmond, a position which gave him the thankless tasks of returning absentees, stragglers, and deserters to their commands, keeping order in the city, guarding Federal captives, and aiding in their exchange. As "detectives" to assist him he hired "plug-uglies" from Baltimore, whose conduct contributed much to Winder's unpopularity in Richmond.[46] Responsibility for issuing passes through the lines was transferred back and forth between the War Department and Winder, who was reproved for granting them too freely. His detectives were accused of furnishing the enemy with crucial information by selling passports for personal profit, and field commanders reached the point where they would not honor Winder's passes.[47] As prisoners left Richmond at the rate of four hundred a day for Andersonville and Macon,* General Winder was placed in charge of all Confederate military prisons in Georgia and Alabama. On June 17, 1864, he assumed command of the post at Andersonville.[48]

* Camp Oglethorpe at Macon was a prisoner-of-war camp for Federal officers.

3

Prison Conditions

THE DAY THAT General Winder took charge at Andersonville was a rainy Friday, the seventeenth consecutive day
the shelterless prisoners had been drenched by showers.[1]
At the beginning of the day 21,539 men huddled together
under leaden skies in the stockade intended for less than half
that number. Three prisoners came in from Charleston during
the day, and the Confederates recaptured eight who had escaped. The small number of prisoners arriving that day was
unusual, the average for June being about 305 daily. The
hospital, which had been moved outside the stockade the latter
part of May, had 1,245 patients that morning, 56 of whom
died during the day.[2] In the stockade were American Indians,
Negroes, representatives of several foreign countries and,
according to a Vermont cavalryman who was there, men from
every state of the Union.[3]

The plight of these unfortunate prisoners was growing
steadily worse. One source of their misery was congestion.
Some relief resulted from moving the hospital outside the
stockade, and the prisoners were not a little pleased to learn,
the day after removal of the hospital began, that the stockade
was to be enlarged.[4] It was easy for Wirz and his associates
to recruit a labor force from among the prisoners for this
work. But instead of following Captain Bowie's suggestion of
constructing a separate stockade on Sweet Water Creek,
which no doubt would better have served the prisoners' needs,
they did what was more convenient and apparently more eco-
nomical. As an extension of the stockade would require erection of only three lines of palisades instead of four, they set

the detail of prisoners to work making a ten-acre addition on the north end of the prison.

This project was not completed until the end of June, by which time the stockade held over twenty-five thousand men.[5] Laborers removed a few palisades from the old north wall, and detachments numbered above forty-nine were ordered into the new addition. Many prisoners had dug wells for water in the original stockade and were reluctant to move where, as one of them put it, "there is no watter or aney thing else & we will have a hard old time until we get some wells dug." A Massachusetts sharpshooter who switched detachments to avoid moving wrote in his diary next day, "The Dutchman that I swapped with has come back to his detachment, and I'm afraid that I shall have to move over into the new stockade, but I shall not until I am obliged to do so." Enlargement of the stockade at least provided more space for a while, but new prisoners arrived steadily, and by the end of July the number in the stockade had reached 29,998.[6]

It is shocking to imagine the discomfort and actual suffering caused by lack of shelter. Many hundreds of prisoners were completely without shelter of any kind to protect them from rain, sun, heat, or cold.[7] Those who had improvised tents, or "shebangs" as they were called by the prisoners, found them inadequate. They were useful in providing shade on hot, sunny days, but their occupants got soaked when it rained. Many prisoners burrowed in the ground for shelter, running the risk of suffocation from cave-ins, and of course their quarters became water holes when heavy rains fell. Others showed great resourcefulness in constructing shelter from the meager materials at their disposal. A Trenton, New Jersey, printer and his friends made an end for their tent by sewing together "the sleeve and back linings of my blouse . . . our sugar and coffee bags, and . . . the flap of Hoffman's knapsack."

Inadequate clothing added to the discomforts of the Andersonville inmates. Men who had been prisoners a long time at Richmond or elsewhere before being sent to Andersonville were clad in tatters when they arrived. Many others came to the prison from the battlefields dressed in garments that gave evidence of rough wear. Prisoners who needed clothing would expect no help from their captors, for the Confederacy could not clothe its own men in the field. Consequently many prisoners suffered from lack of both shelter and clothing. Indeed, some had no clothing at all.[8]

Of the three basic necessities—food, shelter, and clothing —the only one which Confederate authorities provided for the Andersonville prisoners was food. The unsystematic administration of the prison and lack of complete, reliable records make it impossible to obtain precise information about rations, but sufficient evidence is available to prove conclusively that prisoners suffered greatly from dietary deficiencies. The official ration was one-quarter pound of meal and either one-third pound of bacon or one pound of beef, with peas, rice, vinegar, and molasses being issued occasionally.[9] The prison administrators originally intended to issue cooked rations, but cooking and baking facilities were not completed when the first prisoners arrived; by the time they were finished, the stockade contained so many prisoners as to render them grossly inadequate.

When raw rations were issued, prisoners had to have fuel for cooking, and wood soon became scarce in the stockade. As soon as prison officials began to distribute cooked food, they reduced the amount of the ration. An Ohio orderly sergeant complained the first day he drew cooked rations of receiving only a small piece of cornbread and two bites of meat.[10] Sergeant Eugene Forbes of the Fourth New Jersey wrote in his diary on May 30 that his day's ration consisted of "one-third of a loaf of bread, and a piece of bacon about the size of a penny spongecake, one tablespoon of mush." The same day Colonel Persons walked about the stockade and told prisoners that thenceforth full rations would be issued whether or not they were cooked. Henceforth some detachments received cooked rations and some had to cook their own. Each prisoner intermittently drew cooked and raw food.[11]

It was inconceivable that men could long subsist on the rations issued at Andersonville without serious injury to their health. James Selman, Jr., regularly appointed sutler of the post, operated a small market inside the stockade where prisoners who had money could buy vegetables, condiments, cakes, pies, and the like to supplement their diets. The sutler had to pay high prices for his goods, and he sold them at an enormous profit. In April prisoners paid two dollars in United States money for a bunch of four or five green onions. In May black beans were forty cents a pint; molasses, twelve dollars a gallon; corn bread, forty cents a loaf; eggs, fifty cents each; flour, one dollar a pint; dried peas, one dollar a quart; and pork or bacon, six dollars a pound. In June soda sold for twenty-five cents a spoonful; potatoes so small that about sixteen were required to make a quart sold for a dollar and a half a dozen; blackberries sold for sixty cents a pint; and beans had gone up to one dollar a pint.[12] Only those fortunate few who had a large supply of cash could do business with the sutler for any considerable period.

Other ways of getting extra food were to use one's wits in trading or to perform some service for compensation. The prison was alive with hucksters. A prisoner who tented south of the creek commented after a walk along the north side: "It reminds me of Chatham street, New York; it is quite crowded, and the cries of the pedlars are incessantly heard; 'Who wants the wood?' 'Where's the lucky man who will buy the tobacco?' 'Here goes a bully dresscoat, only $4'; 'Here's your good sarsaparilla beer, only ten cents per glass'; 'Who wants the eggs, only 25 cents a piece'; 'Come and get your mustard and soda'; 'Here's your potatoes and squashes'; 'Come on now gentelmen, and give us another bet—here's your chance to double your money,' &c., &c."[13]

Resourceful men dug into the Georgia clay and constructed brick ovens in which they baked better cornbread than came from the bakehouse outside, sold the fruit of their labor, bought the food their bodies craved, and stayed reasonably healthy. Barbers and laundries flourished.[14] Gambling was a source of income for some prisoners who operated chuck-o'-luck wheels or "sweat-boards," where "hundreds of dollars" changed hands daily. Government contractor John Morris of Herkimer County, New York, who had a large sum of money with him when captured at Plymouth, North Carolina, bought up "State money, Savings Bank checks, and other valuable securities for from 50 to 60 cents per dollar."[15] Others were in the same business, and though prisoners who gave up their savings in this way lost money in the long run, they obtained cash for their immediate needs. Trading with the guard was against prison regulations, but guards and prisoners alike paid little attention to the rule.

The benefits to be obtained by these methods were sharply limited. The skillful work of artisans, the acumen of traders, and the machinations of speculators and gamblers were beneficial to scattered individuals but not to the whole body of prisoners. The resources of the men inside the stockade were not sufficient to their needs, and these resources were supplemented, for the most part, only by the daily ration of meal, peas, and bacon or beef. Nearly all the things the prisoners most desired and needed were outside, and the only way to get them was to pay dearly for them. Men were constrained by physical craving to pay unreasonable prices for fresh vegetables and pungent foods. Hence their money, watches, jewelry, and other valuables rapidly passed into the hands of their keepers as compensation for outside edibles. Trades within the stockade might be mutually beneficial to the traders, but they could not add to the prisoners' total stock of goods which was constantly being consumed. As a matter of fact, trading among prisoners often was not mutually advantageous; cunning hucksters were quick to take advantage of inexperienced or less clever comrades. The net result of the prisoners' efforts to improve their lot by their own labor and skill was that some gained at the expense of others.[16]

Prisoners who depended on prison rations fared miserably. A Vermont private described his situation one Sunday, "We get nothing but corn meal & Bacon & we have nothing to cook in but a quart cup for 5 of us & it keeps one of us makeing mush all the time this is a very gay old life where you get your mush for Breakfast mush for Dinner & mush for Supper & nary bit of salt." The following sabbath his ration "consisted of a ½ pint of Boild Rice no meat or bread or meal to go with it." This Vermonter, like other prisoners, preferred uncooked rations because the issue was usually larger, and as a general rule food prepared by the prisoners was more palatable than that cooked outside. His comment on one day's fare was: "the Johneys are giving us cooked Rashions again & they are enough to vomit a Hog for they are not half cooked the Beef & the Rice is sour enough to kill the Devil or aney other tough cuss."[17]

Ohio cavalryman David Kennedy, whose chief complaint at first was the monotony of a diet of fat bacon and cornbread, soon began to deplore the increasing scantiness and inferior quality of his food. On May 23 he wrote: "Rations getting short and very poor. Cornbread, corn ground cob and all." The next day he drew rice which he described as half rice and half dirt, "not half cooked, brought in in an old soap barrel, very strong of soap. enough to make a body puke to look at it." At times prisoners received only one-fourth of a prescribed ration. During the wet month of June rations were sometimes issued in the rain and the food was so soaked that no water had to be added to convert the meal into mush. As the summer wore on, the quality of rations grew poorer and poorer, the monotony of the diet less tolerable, and the complaint of the prisoners more general and persistent. Kennedy wrote in his diary on July 1: "We draw no rations today. Only one ration in three days." On July 2: "This morning we draw rations. Very light. It is composed of a mixture of course corn meal and swamp water, a very little salt half cooked, good to give a hog the colic."[18]

The Fourth of July was a dismal day for Andersonville prisoners, especially for those who had not the means to purchase food. Kennedy observed: "It is a sorrowful Fourth. Hunger gnaws our vitals as we have not drawn any rations for two days. We draw this evening spoilt beef and maggotly mush alive with worms. What a grand dinner for the Fourth." Other prisoners agreed with Kennedy. Ransom August Chadwick, a thirty-one-year-old infantryman from Cattaraugus County, New York, commented: "Rather Dul fourth I tell you shet up in A hog pen Drew fresh Beef or said to be fresh But I called it rather Oald all Magotts and stunk enough to knock a man over this was our fourth supper a grate treate I should reckon after going without Reytions 2 days."

When the Confederate authorities decided to issue uncooked rations, they detailed a crew from among the prisoners to go out under guard each day to cut wood. At first the woodcutting gang consisted of about twenty men; but as the stockade's population steadily increased and the wood nearest the stockade was used up, the size of the fuel detail grew until one hundred troops were required to guard it.[19] The wood used was pitch pine and the smoke from the fires blackened the clothes and skins of the prisoners. Soap, when available at all, was inadequate, and the prisoners found washing without soap to be futile, for "the pitch-pine smoke sticks to both clothes and men like grease." The supply of wood was usually insufficient. Sergeant John M. Burdick, a cavalryman from Greenwich, Washington County, New York, expressed the general sentiment of his comrades when he wrote in his diary, "We don't have wood enough to cook half of what we get." For splitting their meager issue of wood, prisoners were compelled to use such tools as army table knives and railroad spikes.[20]

Prisoners sent out on wood detail frequently took advantage of the carelessness and loose discipline of the guards to make their escape. Consequently an order was issued during the second week of June which required wood squads to take an oath not to attempt to escape. The messes of men violating this oath were to receive no rations until the escapees were recaptured. This threat was not carried out when two woodcutters escaped a short time afterward, but no one was allowed to go out for wood the following two days. On June 17 the entire detail escaped by overpowering the guards and taking their guns, and again the penalty was denial of the wood squad privilege next day. For some time thereafter wood details went out about half the time, and each ten detachments (twenty-seven hundred men) drew one wagonload of wood. Then this issue was doubled and a load was issued to five detachments.[21]

Wood was an important item in the commercial activities of traders in the stockade, and prisoners had ways of getting extra wood from the outside. When they carried sick friends out to the hospital or corpses to the deadhouse, they had the privilege of bringing back all the wood they could carry. When the stockade was enlarged, the prisoners made short shrift of the old stockade wall. One of those left in the older part of the prison wrote in his diary the day after the addition was opened for occupancy: "men going into the new prison choped down the center line of the stockade By star lite"; another who had to move into the new section wrote a day later: "The inner stockade had almost entirely disappeared; the men south of it secured it, as they have all the axes."[22]

Undoubtedly the inmates of Andersonville suffered much from insufficiency of rations and inadequacy of wood for cooking. After almost four months of prison fare one of them expressed his view in the following words: "None will ever realize the suffering here but those that live to endure and live through it. The headquarters of one of the greatest generals [who] ever lived are in here and he is general starvation. Men actually starve to death here for want of food. We are now getting scant rations of beef, some of the wormiest types I ever did see, and one-quarter ration of corn bread, one spoonful of salt a day and not one fifth wood enough to cook with." This prisoner considered his situation no better when next day he got "a change of rations. . . . A pint of cooked beans well seasoned with sand and bugs, a piece of bacon most as large as a walnut and four (4) ounces of corn bread." Hungry men killed low-flying birds and ate them raw as soon as they were dead.[23]

Lack of pure water was also the cause of much suffering. A prisoner who arrived at Andersonville on May 24 observed next day that some prisoners were digging wells, but he and his friends preferred to "use the run water altogether"; he added, "the well water appears impregnated with sulfur, or some mineral, looks blue, and induces diarrhea." But a month later he found the creek water "so coated with grease from the cook house that it is unfit to wash with, much less for drinking." The comment of Private Albert Harry Shatzel, a Vermont cavalryman, was: "not half watter enough to drink & what we do get isn't fit for a Hog for it runs through the camp & every night & morning the cooks empty their greasy watter & filth in the Brook & the stench that arises from the watter is enough to suffocate aney comman man god help us." The water was polluted not only by waste from the cooking and baking establishments but also by two camps of Confederate soldiers located about a quarter of a mile above the stockade, one on each side of the stream. The troops used the stream for bathing and washing clothes, and on its banks were the camp latrines, which overflowed into the creek during heavy rains. Stockade Creek became so contaminated that no one could drink its waters and hope to remain healthy, even if other conditions had been sanitary. A few small springs on the south side of the creek afforded a measure of relief for some of the prisoners, but this supply was limited, and most prisoners relied on wells for water. Some were fortunate enough to obtain tools for this work from prison authorities, but many had to resort to such crude implements as spoons, old fire shovels, or canteen halves.[24]

The whole stockade reeked with an overpowering stench. In the absence of prison discipline, prisoners were very careless of sanitary practices, and men suffering from chronic diarrhea and others too sick to get to the latrines deposited human wastes all over the stockade. An inspecting medical officer "observed men urinating and evacuating their bowels at the very tent doors and around the little vessels in which they were cooking their food. Small pits, not more than a foot or two deep, nearly filled with soft offensive feces, were everywhere seen, and emitted under the hot sun a strong and disgusting odor. Masses of cornbread, bones, old rags, and filth of every description were scattered around or accumulated in large piles."[25] The condition of the stream which was originally intended as the source of water for all needs of the prisoners was appalling. Chief Surgeon Isaiah H. White, reporting on prison sanitation, wrote:

> The margins of the stream passing through the stockade are low and boggy, and having been recently drained, have exposed a large surface covered with vegetable mold to the rays of the sun, a condition favorable to the development of malarious diseases. It is the design of the commandant of the prison to cover the surface with dry sand, but the work has been unavoidably retarded.
>
> The absence of proper sinks (and the filthy habits of the men) have caused a deposit of fecal matter over almost the entire surface of this bottom land.
>
> The point of exit of the stream through the walls of the stockade is not sufficiently bold to permit a free passage of ordure.
>
> When the stream is swollen by rains the lower portion of this bottom land is overflowed by a solution of excrement, which, subsiding and the surface exposed to the sun, produces a horrible stench.[26]

Conditions in the stockade, especially the filth, the stench, and the heat, were very depressing to new arrivals. A prisoner who reached Andersonville on May 22 observed: "such a place I havent had the honor to see before they are Camped in an open field in a hollow where there isn't a breath of air stirring . . . since the day I was Born I never saw such misery as there is here . . . they can't get aney soap or aney thing else to wash their clothes with." Two days later he wrote: "us Boys got a spade & took off the top of the ground & it was alive with maggots where we Lay & the Boys say the ground is so all around here Hard but cant be helped there isn't a Hog stye in the North aney nastier than this camp."[27]

As early as the latter part of March, Michigan cavalryman John L. Ransom noted that the prison was becoming filthy and considered the prisoners themselves "somewhat to blame for it." Before April was half-gone he complained, "There is so much filth about the camp that it is terrible trying to live here." Some attempted to keep clean and to avoid contamination, and on occasion they ducked and scrubbed some of the dirtiest of their comrades, but many quickly became discouraged in these efforts. Clean water soon became scarce, and trying to scrub the smoke of the wood fires off skin or clothes without soap was a hopeless task. Lice and other vermin abounded in the long, uncut, uncombed, matted hair of prisoners. "With sunken eyes, blackened countenances from pitch pine smoke, rags and disease," wrote Ransom, "the men look sickening. The air reeks with nastiness."[28]

"Skirmishing" for lice, or "gray-backs," was a frequent chore. Private Shatzel wrote in his diary on the evening of his second day at Andersonville: "The Boys are all skirmishing for Lice & they are finding them very plenty I think I had better try my Luck." Another prisoner, recording the "lively skirmishing" one day, added: "caught and killed 17 or 20 lice, all fat and in good condition." The prisoners often commented on the size and strength of the lice with commendable good humor. They talked of "gray-back raising" and "louse-fighting," and bragged of the feats of the lice they pretended to be training for exhibition at the next "vermin fair."[29]

Prisoner morale suffered from the seemingly indifferent treatment of the dead. When a man died in the stockade,

other prisoners appropriated whatever possessions he had not
disposed of before expiring and often stripped the body of
its clothes. Then some of them, usually his friends if he had
any, prepared him for burial by placing on his breast a piece
of paper on which were written his name and regiment and
tying his great toes together. They carried the body out to the
deadhouse where corpses were kept while awaiting transportation to the cemetery. The deadhouse was often already full;
at times fifteen or twenty bodies or more had to be left on
the ground outside it. Paroled prisoners carried the corpses
to the cemetery in open wagons, and buried them without
coffins in long, six-feet-wide trenches. They placed the bodies
side by side, touching each other, across the bottom of the
trench, threw in a little earth, laid thick slabs from trunks of
pines over this layer of earth, finished filling the trench, and
erected at each head a stake bearing the name, regiment, and
grave number of the deceased.[30]

The nonchalance with which many regarded death and the
unfeeling eagerness with which they stripped dead or dying
men of their valuables and clothing were shocking to newcomers in the stockade. One disconsolate prisoner thought it
"not very pleasant for a man just breathing his last, and perhaps thinking of loved ones at home who are all so unconscious
of the condition of their soldier father or brother, to be sud-
denly jerked about and fought over, with the cursing and
blaspheming he is apt to hear." An Indiana cavalryman who
arrived at Andersonville in August observed that no more
notice was taken of the dead men in the street each morning
than if they had been swine. So eager were prisoners to take
out bodies and get wood that they sometimes had full-scale
brawls over possession of corpses. A prisoner who had been
at Andersonville about two weeks related: "there was a fellow next to our Tent died & some of the old Prisoners went
through him Like a dose of salts before he had bin dead 5
minits miserable wretches hope to god I may never see sutch
a case again."[31]

An incident recorded by Sergeant Ransom is illustrative
of the callous spirit which pervaded the stockade.

A man caught stealing from one of his comrades and
stabbed with a knife and killed. . . . There were five or

six men stopping together in a sort of shanty. Two of them were speculators and had some money, corn bread, &c., and would not divide with their comrades, who belonged to their own company and regiment. Some time in the night one of them got up and was stealing bread from a haversack belonging to his more prosperous neighbor, and during the operation woke up the owner, who seized a knife and stabbed the poor fellow dead. The one who did the murder spoke out and said: "Harry, I believe Bill is dead; he was just stealing from me and I run my knife into him." "Good enough for him," says Harry. The two men then . . . straightened out "Bill," and then both lay down and went to sleep. . . . This morning poor Bill lay in the hut until eight or nine o'clock, and was then carried outside. The man who did the killing made no secret of it, but told it to all who wanted to know the particulars, who were only a few, as the occurrence was not an unusual one.[32]

It is possible that such occurrences were uncommon, but an abundance of evidence shows that the Andersonville prisoners often treated each other shabbily. One man afflicted with chronic diarrhea soiled his trousers and drawers, which he then washed and left to dry. Someone stole them, leaving the sick prisoner with only a shirt. A sympathetic member of his detachment wrote in his diary that someone gave the victim a pair of drawers, and added: "he now lies near the runlet, his feet awfully swollen, and gradually sinking under disease. Our own men are worse to each other than the rebels are to us."

Conditions at Andersonville were so great a strain on the minds of some men that they lost their sanity. Other prisoners frequently abused and took advantage of these unfortunates. An example was recorded by Sergeant Forbes: "There are quite a number of insane men in camp; one of them has been plundered of everything but his shirt, and while he was asleep, some scoundrel cut off the front tail of that garment, thus leaving him almost without anything to cover his nakedness." The weather was rainy and rather cool, and Forbes thought the poor man "must suffer extremely." Another deranged prisoner had all of his clothing stolen and ran about the stockade completely nude.[33]

Violence among the prisoners was certainly common. One called himself the lightweight champion of Andersonville. Another, after giving an account in his diary of a fight with one of his tentmates, commented: "We have squabbles of this sort often, which don't do any particular harm. Always laugh, shake and make up afterwards." But not all frays ended so harmlessly. In many of them participants were severely injured, and killings were not infrequent. At times the brawling grew to such proportions that the guards became disturbed and began calling their posts each half hour instead of each hour as usual. Private Shatzel wrote in his diary on May 29: "the Boys had another fight and some of them were badly hurt." On June 1: "every thing is very quiet with the exception of now & then a tough old fight between some of the low class of Prisoners here." On the next day: "one of the boys was passing by a tent & a fellow came out & struck him on the Head & killed him." Another prisoner wrote a week later: "there was the most fist fighting I ever saw, bloody fights." Meanwhile another recorded the bucking and gagging of a man by his fellow inmates for knocking his tentmate senseless with a club. Still another expressed surprise that the men in the stockade had become so quarrelsome and belligerent and found it "remarkable how men will stand up and be pummeled."[34]

Under the demoralizing conditions that existed at Andersonville, many prisoners grew very dejected, lost all hope of ever regaining freedom, and resigned themselves to death. Some attempted to find surcease by killing themselves with their own hands. Others sought death by crossing the deadline and inviting a guard to shoot, a method which was not always successful. On July 28 "a man walked outside of dead line, being tired of life, but the guard would not shoot him." But if one were persistent, he might end his suffering by this means. On the night of August 25 a prisoner crossed the deadline, lay down, and ignored the guard's order to get back. When two shots had no effect, the infuriated prisoner told the guard "to 'do his duty. . . .' The third ball penetrated his head." Some prisoners recognized the value of optimism in remaining alive and sustaining health, though a Confederate observer expressed the opinion that the high mortality among the prisoners resulted from "that utter prostration of mind and body which overwhelms the Yankee, but against which the Confederate soldier bears up as bravely as if facing the bullet and bayonet in the field."[35]

The prisoners were prone to blame their Confederate keepers for their sufferings, and Captain Wirz was a very unpopular man among them.[36] But some blamed the United States government for its failure to get them released either by exchange, parole, or rescue. A few days after his arrival at Andersonville Sergeant Kennedy wondered: "What can the Government be thinking of to let their soldiers die in this filthy place." On May 18 he wrote: "Oh, how I wish that some of our rulers could have one week's of our hardship. I think that they would rescue us from here." Two days later: "Can a government exist and let their men die inch by inch here." On May 31 Kennedy thought "that there must be but little feeling manifested in the North for the prisoners." On June 9 he expressed hope of quick parole and added: "I tell you friends it is dreadful here when it is in the power of our Government to release us. . . . we are losing all trust in old Abe."[37]

Kennedy's bitterness increased as conditions at Andersonville grew worse. On June 24 he asked his diary: "Are we brutes or what, that our Government should keep us here to die!" The next day he wrote: "Soldiers that enlisted for their country's cause, true noble boys, reared and bred in homes of plenty here they die of starvation and exposure among the polluted swamps of Georgia. Oh! despotism of the North, can you not send a handful of men to liberate us?" On July 8 new prisoners brought to Andersonville a report that no more exchanges were to take place. Kennedy afterward wrote: "I do not believe it. I do not think that our rulers can be so base to their men. If so, my sincere wish is that our rulers were obliged to come here and stop awhile with us." To other prisoners it seemed that their government was negligent in permitting its men to languish at Andersonville. Sergeant Ransom's view: "our government should get us away from here, and not put objectionable men at the head of exchange to prevent our being sent home or back to our commands." He considered it "a poor government to tie to" if it did not soon arrange deliverance of its soldiers from captivity.[38]

In mid-July a group of prisoners who held similar views got up a petition to the northern people, state governors, and President Lincoln, advising that twenty-five to thirty thousand prisoners were confined at Andersonville, "with daily accessions of hundreds, and that the mortality among them . . . is becoming truly frightful to contemplate, and is rapidly increasing in virulence, decimating their ranks by hundreds weekly," and requesting immediate action to effect their "speedy release, either on parole or by exchange, the dictates both of humanity and justice alike demanding it on the part of our Government." But some took a dim view of the petition. Sergeant Forbes believed "the Government should punish any man who would sign such a document." Private Shatzel was more emphatic: "foolish men," he wrote, "what the hell did they enlist for onley to serve their country & pretect her rights & suffer the consequence, let them be what they will." The sergeants of 107 detachments signed the petition and the Confederate authorities permitted six of them to accompany it to Washington, but nothing came of it.[39]

As week after week passed, the prisoners' situation grew ever more desperate as their number steadily increased and the death rate mounted. So crowded was the stockade that the average amount of space per man for the month of June was only 33.2 square feet. Enlargement of the stockade increased this figure to 40.5 for July, but the constant influx of prisoners reduced it again to 35.7 for August. This was less than four square yards per man, including the uninhabitable swamp. The average number of prisoners during the month of June was 22,291; July, 29,030; and August, 32,899. During the month of June, 1,203 prisoners died; in July, 1,742; and in August, 2,993. The largest number of deaths on any one day was 127 on August 23.[40]

Perhaps it is impossible, as so many ex-inmates maintained, to grasp or convey an accurate picture of the horrors of Andersonville Prison or the suffering endured by the men confined there during that awful summer of 1864. Be that as it may, the comments of observers afford revealing glimpses of existing conditions. Quotations from three eyewitnesses may serve to illustrate. The first was a prisoner who witnessed this scene:

"Three poor mortals breathed their last lying before the Doctor's stand waiting to be prescribed for and died while the rain splattered the sand in their faces." The second was a South Carolinian who wrote his wife, "They [Yankees] have . . . caused us such suffering, and clad every one of our families in mourning, that I feel no pity for them, and behold a dead Yankee in a far different light from a dead Confederate killed in fighting for all that is dear to him." But referring to the stockade, he continued, "It is a singular sight to look down into this inclosure. The suffering within both mind and body is fearful, and one can only compare it to a Hades on Earth. The dirt, filth, and stench in and around the Stockade is awful. I frequently see the Yankees picking from their bodies lice and fleas."[41]

The third eyewitness endured the Andersonville ordeal only to die a few months later in another prison at Florence, South Carolina, of chronic diarrhea and inflammation of the bowels: "One man, who lies near our tent, . . . debilitated with swelled feet from exposure to the sun or dropsy, chronic diarhea, and *neglect of cleanliness,* was found to have the lower part of the body near the rectum eaten into holes by maggots, which literally swarmed on him. He has been washed by some of the men of his detachment, both yesterday and today, but can hardly recover, as there is no prospect of his getting in hospital for some days. By his side lies another who is afflicted in a similar manner, and near him lies one who, although weak from diarrhea, is still able, in a measure, to help himself, but having lost all ambition, has given up hope, and desires only to be left alone to die in his filth. These sights can be seen in any part of the camp and are not isolated cases."[42]

4

Prison Life

THE ABSENCE of facilities for recreation and exercise added to the frustration of life in the Andersonville stockade. It is not surprising that a government which could not provide its prisoners of war with shelter and clothing failed to furnish means for their diversion. Hence the Andersonville prisoners had to amuse themselves as best they could during their leisure hours.

After roll call each morning prison authorities permitted the inmates to do as they pleased so long as they offered no threat of escape. Issuing of rations was time-consuming for sergeants of nineties but not particularly so for others. The police detail engaged a limited number of men, and a few were detailed for outside work such as cooking, baking, burying the dead, cutting wood, clerking, and nursing in the hospital; but the vast majority had to find ways of occupying themselves.

This task was made easier by the lack of necessities and conveniences, which compelled the prisoners to exert themselves to compensate for deficiencies of all sorts. One of the first tasks facing new arrivals, if they were to have any protection from the elements, was construction of huts or "she-bangs." These abodes required constant repairs, and not infrequently prisoners tore down their shelters and rebuilt them in improved style.[1] Shortage of clothing led to consumption of a great deal of time in making and mending clothes. Keeping clean was especially time-consuming because usually no soap was available. Deficiencies in quality and quantity of water made well-digging necessary, and scarcity of proper tools made the task more laborious.[2]

Preparing food used up much time because of the shortage of cooking utensils. Lack of axes and saws made the procurement of wood for cooking and heating a toilsome task. As the death rate increased the prison administrators found it necessary to reorganize the detachments occasionally, taking men from higher-numbered detachments to fill up the ranks of lower-numbered ones which had been depleted. This "squadding over," as the prisoners called it, took all day and was much dreaded by the men because they had to remain in ranks until it was completed. But when they had done all that their captors required of them and all they could do to satisfy their basic physical requirements, many waking hours remained to be filled, and prisoners complained, understandably, of time resting heavily on their hands.[3]

If one may judge from their diaries, the things which interested Andersonville prisoners most were prospects of exchange or parole, rations, the weather, and health. These were the subjects of many conversations while the men lolled about the stockade. New arrivals often busied themselves hatching plans for escape, but in most cases hope of eluding the guards soon waned. When the prison was first established, the Confederates considered it insecure and told their captives that exchange was imminent, hoping thus to deter any outbreak. This was an old story to prisoners coming from Belle Isle and they did not believe it, but their hopes remained alive. When new prisoners arrived, inmates swarmed around them to hear the latest news of exchange or parole as well as to learn about progress of the war and to look for relatives or acquaintances. But the Confederates labored diligently at strengthening the stockade. In early May a prisoner who had arrived at Andersonville in mid-March before the stockade was completed and who had noted the continued efforts to increase its security, expressed doubt that getting out was any longer possible. He added wistfully: "Rebel officers now say that we are not going to be exchanged during the war, and as they can hold us now and no fear of escape, they had just as soon tell us the truth as not, and we must take things just as they see fit to give them to us."[4]

Still, newly arrived prisoners were constantly bringing reports that buoyed the hopes of some. The smallest tidbit of news about exchange was repeated over and over and so liberally embellished that it soon became a general and imminent exchange. Although these rumors always proved false, some prisoners believed them helpful in sustaining life. A realistic outlook is reflected in the observation of the prisoner who wrote: "there is considerable excitement this morning about Paroling, but it is all gass I reckon for there never was so ignorant a lot of men to gether since the World stood that is in reguard to matters outside of the Bull Pen." But this same prisoner did not hesitate to speculate on the state of affairs in the guards' camp. After noting the departure from Andersonville in mid-August of a number of Confederate troops bound for the front, he added, "the Rebs are trying to pull the wool over our eyes by sticking up Notices that there will be a Parole Imidately so as to keep the Boys from making a break dam their lying hearts this isn't the first time we have Guarded our selves since we came into the Bull Pen."[5]

Next to prospects of freedom the most popular topic of conversation among the Andersonville prisoners seems to have been food. They cursed the rations, discussed ways and means of preparing them so as to render them more palatable, and talked over prospects of an improvement in prison fare. Men boasted of the cooking prowess of their wives and mothers and made elaborately detailed plans of the sumptuous feasts they would enjoy on their return home. When food was issued uncooked, groups of prisoners pooled their rations and cooked them together to conserve firewood. Frequently they held animated discussions over the question of how to prepare the food. Some liked to make mush of the meal; some thought dumplings less distasteful; others preferred bread. On occasion they settled the matter by making all three and in addition they would scorch some of the meal and use it as coffee.[6]

When all had made their guesses concerning exchange and parole, the subject of rations was exhausted, and nothing remained to be said about the weather, prisoners frequently turned to discussions of health. They bemoaned the filthy condition of the prison, their own deteriorating health, and the rising mortality rate. Many of them had their own theories about how to avoid sickness. Some thought it extremely important to remain cheerful and to avoid thoughts of home and past pleasures. One prisoner attributed his healthy condition to careful abstinence from tainted food and impure water. Some placed great faith in regular exercise, an occupation which crowded conditions made difficult. A few relied heavily on keeping as clean as possible, others took cathartics, and one confessed, "Why I am sustained is a mystery to me."[7]

Another topic of great interest was the latest reports from the field of battle, and when new prisoners arrived they were swamped with inquiries concerning military activities. New arrivals occasionally brought copies of old newspapers with them, and sometimes Confederate guards gave or sold papers to the prisoners. These papers had wide circulation, and the stockade inmates excitedly discused their contents, scoffing at the prejudiced presentation of news in southern papers. Prisoners frequently heard war news from guards, but they placed little reliance on information from that source. Optimistic rumors of war developments were as wild and unreliable as those concerning exchange. As early as May, 1864, reports circulated in the stockade that Atlanta and Richmond had fallen.[8]

Other subjects were not lacking to engage those inclined to conversation. Some prisoners were so fond of relating past experiences that their life histories became well known, and acquaintances tired of hearing the same stories repeated. Sailors told tall stories of the sea; foreigners and others who had traveled in distant lands described alien places and people and customs. Some demonstrated their vituperative talents in denouncing the South in general and the keepers of Andersonville Prison in particular. Still others seemed unable to converse without speaking longingly of loved ones at home. Another topic which absorbed the attentions of many prisoners was the possibility of escape.[9]

During the existence of Andersonville Prison 329 prisoners escaped; a far greater number got away temporarily but were recaptured. Permanent escape was rendered exceedingly difficult by the remoteness of Andersonville from Union lines and the efficiency of the dogs which Confederates used to track runaways.[10] Most of the prisoners who escaped did so by running off from outside work details or by violating their paroles while employed outside the stockade. Some got away by bribing guards, others simply by walking off after returning tools from the stockade at the end of the day. But for the vast majority of prisoners the only hope of escape seemed to be through tunneling, and to this activity they devoted much time and effort.

When a group of prisoners decided to engage in a "tunnel operation," they tried to get a spot near the deadline from which to begin. If they had quarters large enough to permit, they might start digging under their shelter. If not, they pretended to be in search of water and after digging a "well" struck out horizontally from its side. Seriously handicapped by lack of tools, they were forced to use such implements as sharp sticks, knives, and canteen halves. A group of tunnelers who obtained an old fire shovel considered themselves very fortunate. Only one man at a time could dig in the narrow burrow, and progress was very slow. As the tunnel lengthened, men lined up behind the digger to pass back the loosened earth, which was surreptitiously dumped in the creek. When the tunnel's owners considered it long enough to open, they chose their night to go through; after their passage, any other prisoners who desired to do so might use the tunnel. The more men getting out, the greater the chance of confusing the dogs and enabling the first ones through the tunnel to make good their escape.[11]

Tunneling was a hazardous venture. Digging was difficult to conceal and detection led to serious punishment. The soil was subject to cave-ins. If one got out through a tunnel, he ran the risk of being shot or, if recaptured, having to wear a ball and chain or being put in the stocks or on a chain gang. On one occasion some prisoners had completed a long tunnel and were preparing to break out when a cave-in trapped the sergeant who had gone to open the tunnel. According to a member of the sergeant's mess, "he had to dig out & when he came out the Reb guard took him down to Hd Qr's & now he is in the stocks hard but honest." Four days later this philosophical diarist recorded the opening of another tunnel and added: "100 of the Boys left last night & 2 more were going out this morning & they were shot poor Boys such is life some die one way & some another."[12]

Another prisoner wrote after the recapture and return of several men who had been out about twelve days: "they all have balls and chains; there must be now nearly 100 men wearing these articles." But at least one of those condemned to wear the ball and chain for attempting to escape was able to deceive the Confederates. As soon as they returned him to the stockade and departed, he lost himself in the crowd and removed the ball and chain. Thereafter he wore the shackles only when reporting to the gate each morning at nine o'clock for inspection.[13]

After involvement in a tunneling project which was abandoned because "the location was not practicable," Sergeant Ransom joined another group of tunnelers. The second venture was successful and the cavalryman went out with a friend one dark night shortly before daylight. When the two had crawled some 200 or 250 yards from the stockade, they were startled by the guards firing at other prisoners coming out the tunnel. They jumped up and ran, "seemingly making more noise than a troop of cavalry." When the first light appeared in the east, they had traveled only about three miles, were covered with mud and scratches, and could hear the yelping dogs on their trail. Ransom afterward wrote: "In a few moments the hounds came up with us and began smelling of us. . . . did not offer to bite us." Soon five mounted Confederates arrived and escorted the forlorn prisoners back to the prison to see Captain Wirz. "After cursing us a few minutes," wrote Ransom, "we were put in the chain gang, where we remained two days." Although the chain gang was not exactly pleasant, he found it "not so bad after all. We had more to eat than when inside," he added, "and we had shade to lay in, and although my ankles were made very sore, do not regret my escapade."[14]

The prison-keepers frequently sent Negroes into the stockade to check the wells and search for tunnels which, when found, had to be dug out and filled in. Apparently, the Negroes were not greatly interested in discovering tunnels, or the prisoners were remarkably clever in concealing them. On July 20 a prisoner wrote: "A tunnel was opened this A.M., about two o'clock, and men were escaping until after daylight, when the guard discovered them and gave the alarm." Though Negroes probed wells and looked for more tunnels that day, a group of prisoners opened another one after dark. But no one escaped on this occasion. In their eagerness to get out, about five hundred men congregated near the tunnel entrance, arousing the suspicions of the guards and defeating their own purpose. Some of the guards were deficient in vigilance and a few of them helped prisoners to escape. The stockade inmates noted one night that seven sentry posts were silent. Next day a prisoner recorded in his diary: "this morning it was ascertained that fourteen of our men had 'tunneled out,' and that seven guards had accompanied them, taking their arms and accoutrements."[15]

On the other hand, some tunnel projects were thwarted by traitors or "turncoats" among the prisoners themselves. Psychological and medical studies of the effects of confinement and dietary deficiencies on the behavior of prisoners in World War II and the Korean conflict help to explain disloyalty at Andersonville. These studies show that human life requires the maintenance of a satisfactory body temperature, adequate intake of food, fluids, and air, satisfactory elimination of wastes, a satisfactory amount of rest and activity, and satisfactory relationships with other human beings. Failure to meet these conditions results in various physical discomforts and in fear, anxiety, anger, loneliness, sadness, and dejection. Men placed in a situation like Andersonville Prison, which upsets these relationships and produces extreme pressures, sometimes follow a pattern of reaction which culminates in exasperation, dejection, and unreasoning dependence upon any offer of help. In this condition, which psychologists call "situation of frustration," a man is "emotionally bankrupt," at the "end of his rope," and unusually receptive to approval or human support. He will do anything to win approval of those human beings in whose power he finds himself. Deprivation of food contributes directly to this "situation of frustration."[16] Considering the conditions that existed in the stockade, it is not surprising that some prisoners did become informers.

"Tunnel-traitors" were useful to the Confederates and a

thorn in the side of fellow-prisoners. It was not unusual for a tunnel to be reported just when its diggers were ready to reap the fruit of their labors. On one occasion in mid-June some thirty prisoners were prepared to open their tunnel when one of their number betrayed them. Shortly afterward one of the disappointed conspirators wrote in his diary: "the devil is to pay again for the Rebel Serg't found the Tunnel where a 200 of us was going out to Night god help the man that informs on this party if he is found he is going up the first pot sure."[17]

Nor was this an idle threat, for informers, when caught, received rough treatment at the hands of fellow-prisoners. A New York cavalry sergeant wrote in mid-July, "Today a tunnel was discovered by the rebel authorities, 4 of the prisoners had dug a well 60 feet deep, about 20 feet down they had struck out dug 20 feet outside the stockade and were a going to escape in 10 nights, one of our men betrayed them for a plug of tobacco." A New Jersey infantry sergeant recorded the same incident, adding that other prisoners shaved the hair off half the traitor's head, branded the letter "T" on his forehead, and marched him about the camp for all to see.[18] A Michigan cavalry sergeant wrote of an informer whose punishment was more serious: "A lame man, for telling of a tunnel, was pounded almost to death last night, and this morning they were chasing him to administer more punishment, when he ran inside the dead line claiming protection of the guard. The guard didn't protect worth a cent, but shot him through the head. A general hurrahing took place, as the rebel had only saved our men the trouble of killing him."[19]

The number of traitors in the stockade was large enough to render impracticable any organized plan of escape involving a large number of prisoners. In late May a plot was devised to execute a grand break by undermining the stockade so that at a given signal the conspirators could rush forward and push over several palisades, capture the batteries, overpower the guard, and release the other prisoners. It was a daring plan, possibly a foolhardy one; but at that time the Confederate regulars had recently left Andersonville for Richmond, and the prison was guarded by undisciplined reserves whom many prisoners expected to abandon their posts and take to the woods at the first sign of a determined uprising. But the break was not made. A traitor disclosed the plot to prison authorities, who had the tunnels destroyed, and to discourage any outbreak Captain Wirz had the following notice posted inside the stockade: "Not wishing to shed the blood of hundreds not connected with those who concocted a plan to force the stockade, and make in this way their escape, I hereby warn the leaders and those who formed themselves into a band to carry out this, that I am in possession of all the facts, and have made arrangements accordingly, so to frustrate it. No choice would be left me but to open with grape and canister on the stockade, and what effect this would have in this densely crowded place need not be told."[20]

In mid-July Wirz summoned the sergeants of messes to his headquarters and informed them that though his government was eager to exchange prisoners, the United States would not do so because the enlistment terms of many Federal prisoners had expired. Assuring them that he had plenty of rations to feed them two years if necessary, Wirz warned the prisoners that an attempted break would be suicide. In the words of Sergeant Forbes, he "stated that . . . if the attempt were made, he would open on the stockade with grape and canister so long as a man were left alive within it." Such threats made some prisoners apprehensive. About two o'clock that afternoon Confederate artillerymen fired two cannon as a signal for guards to man their stations and demonstrate how well prepared they were to repel an uprising. Many prisoners thought it was the beginning of a massacre. Forbes afterward wrote: "sergeants engaged in issuing rations, dropped their cups or knives, and fell flat to the ground, rooting their noses into mother earth like babies for their 'titty,' men plunged headlong into the 'dug out' tents, the brook, or any place that offered the least show, or, in fact, no show for shelter against the storm of grape and canister which they expected was soon to come hurtling over their devoted heads; cries of 'lie down' and other vociferations resounded through all parts of the camp, and the writer hereof felt very much as if he would as soon be somewhere else, to say the very least."[21]

An Illinois cavalryman wrote fifteen years later that the

cannon firing "was answered with a yell of defiance from ten thousand throats," and that the prisoners stood "erect, excited, defiant." Perhaps a fairly accurate idea of their reaction may be gotten from the diary of a prisoner who wrote: "The Rebbs tried to show us how smart they Could be shot 12 lb guns (as a signal; it took them ½ hour to fall in) we could take all they have got here in half that time   they scared some of our boys half to Death while others called the rebbs every thing they Could and laughed at them and they soon played out."[22]

Apparently some of the guards, as well as residents of the neighborhood, were not informed of the drill, for according to one prisoner, "as soon as the alarm was given, they commenced 'skedaddling' for the woods, making as good time as a quarter horse." Prisoners also observed women and children fleeing from nearby houses into the woods. After some thirty minutes of tumult, "everything relapsed into the usual state of semi-confusion." The drill, insofar as it was intended to impress the prisoners, was not very successful. One private wrote: "The Johneys . . . fired their Artillery & raised the devil generaly for a spell then returned to their Qr's & all they can muster hear is about 2500."[23]

Prisoners had a very low opinion of the Georgia Reserves. Relations between captives and captors, which prior to replacement of Confederate regulars at Andersonville by reserves had been as pleasant as could be expected under the circumstances, deteriorated rapidly when the undisciplined recruits took over. One prisoner, after describing the suffering he endured en route to Andersonville, wrote: "we are under the Malishia & their ages range from 10 to 75 years & they are the Dambdst set of men I ever have had the Luck to fall in with yet . . . God help the Prisoner when they fall into the hands of the Malishia." Another wrote that "perched upon the stockade as guards" were "the worst looking scallawags . . . from boys just large enough to handle a gun, to old men who ought to have been dead years ago for the good of their country." A third characterized his guards as "the off scourings of the South," and added, "They act as though they were scared to death at the sight of a Yankee." According to a fourth, some sentries on duty in late July were barely able to see over the stockade, "being 14 or 15 years old and very small."[24]

Prisoners were especially critical of the alacrity with which the reserves fired on men crossing or reaching over the deadline. So trigger-happy were some of the sentinels that their captives believed the false rumor that guards received a thirty-day furlough for each Yankee whom they killed. Of course the prisoners were prejudiced in their judgments, but the testimony of Confederate observers substantiates both the unsoldierly qualities of the reserve troops and their excessive zeal for shooting. Captain Wirz complained of their "carelessness" and "inefficiency" and asserted that their "worthlessness" was "on the increase day by day." General Winder bemoaned their lack of discipline and reported to Richmond that he could not depend on them. Charles H. Thiot, a Chatham County, Georgia, planter, serving as an enlisted man in the First Georgia Regiment, wrote his wife that some reserves had "no more sense than to shoot them [prisoners] if they dare cross the line just to pick up a ball or empty a washpan." Subsequently he wrote: "some of them would like nothing better than to shoot one of the scoundrels just for the fun of it. Indeed I heard one chap say that he just wanted one to put his foot over the line when he was on post, and he would never give him time to pull it back. Many would murder them in cold blood."[25]

One member of the reserves, Private James E. Anderson, was so distressed by the frequent shootings at the deadline that he wrote the following complaint to President Jefferson Davis: "We have many thoughtless boys here who think the killing of a Yankee will make them great men. . . . every day or two there are prisoners shot. When the officer of the guard goes to the sentry stand, there is a dead or badly wounded man invariably within their own lines. The sentry, of course, says he was across the dead-line when he shot him. . . . Last Sabbath there were two shot in their tents at one shot. The boy said that he shot at one across the deadline. Night before last there was one shot near me (I being on guard). The sentry said that the Yankee made one step across the line to avoid a mud hole. He shot him through the bowels, and when the officer of the guard got there he was lying inside their own lines. He (the sentry) as usual told him that he stepped across, but fell back inside."[26]

The Sunday shooting of two men in a tent to which Anderson referred occurred on June 19. Sergeant Forbes, who recorded the incident in his diary, averred that a prisoner obtained permission of the sentry to cross the deadline for the purpose of killing a snake and that another guard fired from a distant post, missed the snake-killer, and injured two men in a tent, one in the head, the other in the thigh.

Private Shatzel wrote on June 22: "there was 3 men shot dead last night & there wasn't one of them inside of the dead line." On another occasion Forbes wrote of a guard firing at a prisoner who pushed a piece of wood over the deadline and added that the "rebel sergeant told the sentry he was a fool and never did know his business." One sentinel accidentally fired his gun and hit a prisoner who was in the act of taking his pipe from his mouth, cutting his thumb, finger, cheek, and tongue. Another shot himself by accident. Firing by sentinels was very common indeed, especially at night, but many of the shots did no physical damage.[27]

Occasionally citizens of the region, both male and female, came to visit the prison and to get a look at the "Yanks." A prisoner observed "sympathy in some of their faces and in some a lack of it." Among these visitors were members of the Americus Ladies Aid Society, who went to Andersonville to carry food to sick Confederate soldiers. While there they visited the cemetery to watch the burial of dead Federals and climbed the sentry box ladders to gaze down upon the unfortunate prisoners. These ladies grieved over the sick and dying soldiers of the Confederacy, but the sympathy of some did not extend to the stockade inmates. One young beauty who went up to see the Yankees was Miss Hallie Clayton of Americus. A woman who accompanied her wrote sixty-five years later that Miss Clayton "was disposed to say ugly things to them & glory at their being captured, and imprisoned." Visitors declined in number with the passing of time as few were willing to endure the stench which eventually enshrouded the stockade.[28]

Prison life would have been less dreary for many if reading material had been plentiful, but those who wished to read

had little or no choice. Bibles and New Testaments seem to
have outnumbered all other books combined within the stockade, and many inmates found a measure of solace in perusing
the Scriptures. Charles Ross, of Lower Waterford, Vermont,
wrote in his diary one Saturday: "Have read a good lot in
the Bible today. Am not through with the book of Isiah. I
am getting more proffit from such reading than a little." Another Vermonter wrote August 30: "finished reading the
Testament for the first time in my Natchrel life," and the
next day started it again. Perhaps the most sought-after reading matter was newspapers, especially from the North, but
they were few and far between. Illinois Cavalryman John
McElroy wrote years later that the only thing he could get
to read was a copy of *Gray's Anatomy*. Other prisoners
managed to obtain a *History of America*, Milton's *Paradise
Lost*, and Bunyan's *Pilgrim's Progress*.[29]

Mail, the reading matter which would have afforded the
greatest pleasure, was exceedingly scarce. Prisoners were permitted to write one-page letters. They received both correspondence and packages, but deliveries were very infrequent,
and all mail was carefully censored. Outgoing letters informed
the recipient of the prisoner's whereabouts and gave assur-
ances of his well-being. Some writers gave the place and date
of their capture or the names of other Andersonville prisoners
known to the addressee. One stated that writing news was
not permitted and that if it were, he had none to write.
Another instructed his parents: "Write . . . nothing but
family matters and no longer than I have written. leave the
envelope open so to be Inspected by the Confederate authorities." A foreign-born member of a New York regiment wrote
his brother: "tha donet low us to Rite Only So much Right
as Son as you Can and in Ingles Becos tha Rede Ol the latars
Befor we git tham."[30]

A Michigan cavalry sergeant who had reasonably good
penmanship was importuned by his fellow inmates to write
letters to Wirz, General Winder, President Davis, and other
Confederate officials describing the woeful circumstances of
individual prisoners and begging for release. A Pennsylvania
cavalryman paroled as hospital steward managed, "through
the kindness of a friend," to send an uncensored letter. He

wrote: "Don't be uneasy about me. I am going to live it through—about 12,000 of our brave boys died in this place this summer. . . . You can judge how they must be situated and treated. I will some day be able to tell you all about it." Another Pennsylvanian, S. J. Gibson, whose letter was passed by the censor, contrived to make it clear that Andersonville was difficult to endure. He wrote his wife: "it is my misfortune still to be held a Prisoner of War; Our condition is by no means a desirable one; . . . We try to be as cheerful and contented as we can, . . . Give yourself no uneasiness concerning *me*; I can live where any other man can."[31]

Correspondence consumed relatively little of the Andersonville prisoners' time, and in the struggle with ennui they turned to various other activities. To avoid having to draw rations in caps or shoes, those who could get old pieces of stovepipe or tin twisted them into dishes. Many carved wooden spoons. One prisoner later wrote that he and a friend carved chess pieces out of roots from the swamp, blackened one set with soot, obtained a wide plank which was usable as a board, and found in playing chess a way of temporarily forgetting some of the misery surrounding them. Some spent much time visiting and ministering to sick prisoners. Others took frequent walks looking for old acquaintances or merely observing life in the stockade. A prison diarist reported seeing small gardens of beans and corn, no more than three inches wide, planted around three sides of some tents. A Michigan printer enjoyed spreading his ration of cow peas out on a blanket and picking them up one by one as fast as he could, as if picking up type. One hindrance to this pastime was his habit of unconsciously putting the peas in his mouth. "In this way," he wrote, "I often eat up the whole printing office." He found another printer in prison and the two sometimes had "pea-picking" contests. Some prisoners occupied themselves by carving ornaments from bone or wood with knives made from iron hoops. Others drew sketches with rude pens dipped in ink made from rust.[32]

Andersonville had no chaplain, but some of the prisoners held religious services on their own. In May Reverend William John Hamilton, a Catholic priest who lived in Macon and whose mission included all of southwestern Georgia, visited Andersonville; finding a very large number of Catholic prisoners there, he asked the bishop of Savannah to send priests to minister to them. He returned the following week and spent three days giving to Catholic inmates the consolations of their religion. In June Bishop Augustin Verot of Savannah sent another priest, Reverend Peter Whelan, to minister to prisoners who paid allegiance to the Roman Catholic Church. Finding himself unable to attend to their spiritual needs, Father Whelan wrote to Savannah for help and the bishop sent Father Claveril to assist him.[33]

The priests won the sincere admiration of most prisoners, of whatever faith. One inmate observed that smallpox cases received the same attention as any others. "They [the priests] are in every day," another wrote, "and are the only Christian professors who visit the camp." The holy fathers frequently had to get down on hands and knees and crawl into dugouts and hear confessions or administer extreme unction while lying alongside sick or dying prisoners. Some non-Catholic residents of the countryside were shamed because none of their clergy visited the prison, and prisoners inquired of the priests the cause of this negligence. Addressing himself to this question, Bishop Verot, who twice visited the stockade himself, wrote that "error, sterile by its nature, will not produce the rush of charity proportionate to the extent of the needs."[34]

Father Claveril soon fell ill and retired to Father Hamilton's residence in Macon to recover. Father John Kirby came from Augusta to replace him, but stayed only about two weeks. According to Father Hamilton, one "could find every nationality inside the stockade," and the clergymen were disturbed by their inability to communicate with prisoners who could not understand English. After Father Kirby's departure a Jesuit from Spring Hill College near Mobile, Alabama, Father Hosannah, who could speak a number of languages, came to Andersonville. He and Father Whelan remained until near the end of September, when most of the prisoners had been removed. As a result of the labors of these devoted men, the Savannah bishop was able to proclaim that "many Protestants and many unbelievers had the good fortune of conversion to our holy religion and received baptism."[35]

A Methodist missionary to Florida troops in the Confederate army, Reverend E. B. Duncan, addressed the Andersonville prisoners on two occasions. Visiting the post in early August for the purpose of expounding the gospel to the company of Florida artillery stationed there, Duncan delivered a sermon in the stockade from atop a box near the sutler's stand. Again in January, 1865, when only about five thousand captives remained at Andersonville, he stopped on his way to Florida and spent three evenings conducting religious services for the Confederate troops. Before leaving he preached to the stockade inmates and briefly to the patients in the prison hospital. Of his second adventure in the stockade, Duncan wrote to a fellow minister: "They stood up round me, while I stood on a box and declared to them the Gospel. . . . I had unusual liberty, and they listened with most profound attention. At the close I invited them to seek religion and come to God, when the ground was literally covered with them that prostrated themselves. But few in that vast assembly remained standing. . . . They treated me with the greatest respect, thanking me kindly and begging me to return, and followed me when leaving as if loath to let me go. Many came to shake hands, until, like the Indian, I said, 'I shake hands in my heart.' "[36]

During the spring of 1864 a few prisoners started holding prayer meetings and attempting to preach, and by mid-July these meetings had attracted a large following. It became more or less customary to hold prayer meetings and preaching services on alternate nights. These gatherings had no fixed location. At dusk the song leaders would go to the spot decided upon for that particular night and start some familiar hymn, whereupon interested prisoners would assemble. T. J. Shepherd, an Ohio prisoner who did a good deal of the preaching, later estimated that possibly a hundred men were converted as a result of meetings with which he was connected. Also active in the services was Boston Corbett, later famous as slayer of John Wilkes Booth. Prominent song leaders were Sergeant B. N. Waddell of Kenton, Ohio, David Atherton of New York, and J. C. Turner of Townline, Lucerne County, Pennsylvania. In addition to prayer meetings and preaching services, pious prisoners also conducted funeral ceremonies, formed an organization to care for the sick, and met on Sunday mornings to study the Bible in an "Andersonville Sunday School." When a heavy August rain opened a fresh spring of water just inside the west deadline a short distance north of the creek, many prisoners considered it the result of divine intervention in answer to their prayers, and called the fount "Providence Spring."[37] Present-day visitors to Andersonville Prison Park may still drink of its cool, free-flowing water.

5

The Raiders

A MONG THE ANDERSONVILLE prisoners was a large group
of thieves, robbers, and murderers, who contributed
heavily to the woes of their fellow-inmates.* The ravages of these "Raiders" provided a convincing demonstration
of the imperative need for law and order among men. As
unmolested highwaymen of the Middle Ages struck fear into
the hearts of unprotected travelers, the Andersonville Raiders
terrorized the stockade until they became the most dreaded
horror of prison life. At first the Raiders were merely a small
number of cutthroats and petty criminals who had been attracted to military service by the rewards of bounty-jumping
and had been captured before they could collect their bounties
and find an opportunity to desert. Some of the other prisoners
had made their acquaintance at Belle Isle where they had
been imprisoned before their removal to Andersonville. This
nucleus of recruits from the underworld grew into a formid-
able force of ruffians and robbers which eventually numbered
four or five hundred. Imprisonment of other thugs swelled
the Raiders' ranks, as did the degeneration of formerly up-
right men who succumbed to the temptation to partake of the
fruits of robbery. This consideration was a strong incentive
indeed, for the Raiders' standard of living was superior to
that of other prisoners, and fear of punishment, which in
organized society may act as a deterrent to crime, was incon-
sequential.

The Raiders were divided into groups under the leadership

* For material in this chapter the writer has drawn freely from his "Andersonville Raiders," *Civil War History*, II (1956), 47–60.

of various "chieftains," among whom were Charles Curtis,
Fifth Rhode Island Artillery, John Sarsfield, One-hundred-
forty-fourth New York, Patrick Delaney, Eighty-third Penn-
sylvania, and William Collins, Eighty-eighth Pennsylvania.
The henchmen of each leader were designated by the chief-
tain's name, such as "Collins' Raiders" or "Curtis' Raiders."
Collins was also called "Mosby" and his followers "Mosby's
Raiders" after the famous Confederate Ranger, John S.
Mosby. It was this comparison with cavalry raiders which
led to application of the term "Raiders" to the prison hoodlums. Sergeant Ransom, who was in the same detachment as
Collins, wrote in his diary: "Capt. Moseby, of the raiders,
is . . . quite an intelligent fellow and often talks with us. We
lend him our boiling cup which he returns with thanks. Better
to keep on the right side of him, if we can without countenanc-
ing his murderous operations."[1]

Another Raider chief was Cary Sullivan, Company F, Sev-
enty-sixth New York, who was described by a comrade as
"a substitute from Buffalo—a gambling, fighting, bad tem-
pered fellow in the Company." Sullivan deserted on the night
of October 10, 1863, while his regiment was preparing for
action near the Rapidan River. Captured by Confederate cavalry, he was imprisoned for a time at Belle Isle where he
was credited with being "the means of many deaths," and
later was transferred to Andersonville. Some members of his
old regiment were captured near Chancellorsville the following spring and arrived in the stockade May 24, 1864. Among
them was John Worrell Northrop, who wrote in his diary
about three weeks later: "Soon after we came in we were
told that one of a gang of thieves went by the name of Cary.
. . . Today he was pointed out to us and we recognized Sullivan of our Co." Aware that he was recognized, Sullivan sent
word that night that Company F would not be bothered by
Raiders if its members would not expose him as a deserter.
A few days later, in conversation with the company's orderly
sergeant, G. W. Mattison, he denied having anything to do
with the Raiders, but not expecting to be believed, he continued to instruct his emissary to assure the Company F men
that he would use his influence as a chief to prevent the robbers from molesting them. On June 28 Northrop wrote:

"Some days since Mooney's blanket was Stolen. He appealed to this old acquaintance with threats and promises & Sullivan brought back the identical blanket."[2]

Among prisoners taken at Olustee, Florida, who arrived at Andersonville about the middle of March, were numerous reinforcements for the Raiders. Many of them were ruffians who had enlisted in the Seventh New Hampshire because of the large state bounty. They had received their bounties and tried to desert, but the United States Army had literally kept them under guard and had actually sent some to the regiment in chains. They deserted to the Confederates in the retreat from Olustee. These rogues were typical Raiders.

At first the marauders contented themselves with petty thievery carried out under cover of darkness. Occasionally other prisoners would catch a Raider and punish him by bucking and gagging, shaving his head, or riding him on a rail. But such punishment seemed a small price to pay for the benefits to be gained by plundering, and the Raiders' temerity increased as they grew stronger and better disciplined. Prison authorities made no attempt to interfere with them and the other prisoners had no organization for dealing with the problem. New prisoners with good clothes, blankets, jewelry, and money were the favorite prey of the ruffians. One prisoner wrote in his diary the day after his arrival at Andersonville: "The cry of 'raiders' awoke us last night & we remembered what we had been told by some of the old prisoners yesterday, about thieves—a set of brutal men who steal everything possible, & even robbed men of money & watches & in some cases brutally beating men so they die from the cause. They boldly take blankets from over men's heads standing over them with clubs, threatening to kill them if they move. They are regularly organized bandit bands led by the most desperate characters. Here they bear the name of Raiders. Going among the men of our Company we find they had not fully realized this unexpected danger & some had lost boots, knapsacks containing all they have, blankets, canteens, dishes, their small stock of provisions &c. In other parts we hear of pocket picking, assaults with clubs & this is the work of every night especially after new arrivals."[3]

These "bandit bands" prowled the prison looking for victims, often attacking a tent and taking all the possessions of its occupants, including the clothes from their backs. Surplus goods they traded to the guards. The advantage of organization was demonstrated when other prisoners came to the assistance of the victims. "Occasionally," wrote Sergeant Ransom, "a party of new comers stick together and whip the raiders, who afterward rally their forces and the affair ends with the robbers victorious." These fights sometimes created such a stir that the guards became alarmed and stopped the melee by threatening to fire on the crowd.[4]

One night some prisoners caught a thief in the act of stealing a pair of shoes and tied him up, intending to punish him after daylight. A fellow-hoodlum freed him, but the next morning he was found and recaptured, "knocked down three times, sopped in the filthy ditches of the swamp, . . . marched about the camp, [and] given seven lashes on the bare back." A New York infantryman recording the incident in his diary described the villain as "a squalid looking chap with the head of an ape." A search among known pilferers for stolen articles and money turned up several items before "a dozen savage fellows came on the crowd with clubs. A few stood & fought them with their hands but were badly beaten and forced to yield."[5]

The Raiders constantly improved their system. After carefully selecting a victim, they snatched away his possessions, clubbed any friends who tried to assist him, and fled. Ransom noted: "Raiders getting more bold. . . . Often rob a man now of all he has, in public, making no attempt at concealment." They pounced on new prisoners as soon as they were fairly within the gate. About two thousand of these who arrived in early May provided excellent picking for the robbers. Captured at the siege of Plymouth, North Carolina, they had just received their veteran bounties and soon would have been sailing for home had their garrison not been attacked. Dressed in stylish new uniforms and carrying well-filled knapsacks, the "Plymouth Pilgrims" had in their possession a large sum of money when they reached Andersonville. Kindly appearing men offered to show the unsuspecting newcomers where they could sleep, then robbed them during the night. If a victim resisted he was likely to have his throat slashed or his skull

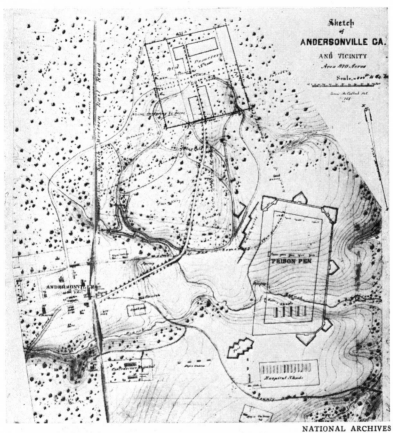

Map marking off the dimensions and placement of Andersonville Prison, near Americus, Georgia. Date on the drawing says 1868, which would be after the camp closed.

Andersonville Prison, August 17, 1864. Prisoners followed whims in locating and building their huts. This failure of prison authorities to lay off streets and have prisoners construct their quarters in rows was a tragic omission. It resulted in the above pictured hodgepodge of structures which contributed to much of the misery, stench, and disorder prevalent at the prison.

Andersonville Prison, August, 1864. Issuing rations was a main event in the dreary prison life although many prisoners had to cook their own food.

Andersonville Prison, summer, 1864. In the foreground the open latrine, and running beside it the camps' supply of water which collected unimaginable filth.

A view of Andersonville Prison, 1864, showing the famous deadline which meant death to any prisoner who crossed it.

NATIONAL ARCHIVES

Burying the dead at Andersonville Prison, summer, 1864. Prisoners carried the corpses to the cemetery in open wagons, and buried them without coffins in long six-foot-wide trenches, placing the bodies side by side. Some 13,000 Union prisoners died at the prison between February 24, 1864, and May 5, 1865.

The plaque reads:

Captain Henry Wirz, under the immediate command of Brigadier-General John H. Winder, C.S.A., absent on sick leave, August 1864, commanded the inner prison at Camp Sumter, April 12, 1864 to May 7, 1865. To the best of his ability he tried to obtain food and medicine for Federal prisoners and permitted some to go to Washington in a futile attempt to get prisoners exchanged. He was tried for failure to provide food and medicines for Federals imprisoned here—though his guards ate the same food—and mortality was as high among Confederate guards as among prisoners. Of him, Eliza Frances Andrews, Georgia writer, said, "Had he been an angel from heaven, he could not have changed the pitiful tale of privation and hunger unless he had possessed the power to repeat the miracle of the loaves and fishes." Refusing to implicate others, he gave his life for the South, November 10, 1865.

Graves of the six infamous Andersonville Raiders, about 150 feet inside Andersonville Cemetery entrance. These men and their some 50 followers terrorized the prison camp, killing and stealing from their fellow prisoners, until finally the six were tried, found guilty of murder, and hanged on July 10, 1864.

crushed. As raiding parties became more frequent, the number of battles increased. If the Raiders were able to obtain their loot before the alarm was given, they ran away. If not they signaled for aid and fought back.

The predators enjoyed certain advantages which discouraged resistance. Being better fed, they were stronger physically. While other prisoners died of starvation, scurvy, diarrhea, and dysentery, the Raiders had green beans, onions, potatoes, flour, and fresh meat, obtained by purchase or barter from the sutler or guards. They were well-organized and accustomed to brawling. In a fight involving large numbers of men their familiarity with each other was assurance against striking a friend, whereas in the confusion their opponents were apt to attack allies and foes with equal vigor. The raiders were also better armed. In addition to clubs, many of the spoilers carried such weapons as axes, "slung-shots," brass knuckles, and Bowie knives. With such advantages on the side of the Raiders, other prisoners were reluctant to resist their brazen pillage.

Realizing the situation, the hoodlums pursued their advantages to the full. In mid-June a prisoner wrote: "Suspicious looking chaps move thro' different parts of the prison. Presently the Cry of 'thief' 'raiders' and supressed voices are heard like men in a struggle—Again cries of 'Catch him' 'Murder' 'Oh God! they've killed me!' Now & then one is Caught & cries & begs most dolefully. Then squads of twenty strong, Savage looking men run thro' the streets with clubs & soon there is a desperate fight. The blows are plainly heard & Savage oaths & cries of fright and distress. Then for a time the desperadoes vanish. The disturbance kept up all night So we did not feel safe to lie down unless some one of our tent watched. I . . . have seen some who 'got hit.' Some Massachusetts boys near us had their blanket taken from them."[6] Two days later another prisoner noted that raiding was becoming more extensive. That night the Raiders were on the prowl again. The next morning about eleven o'clock they knocked a man down and took his watch and eighty dollars.

Sergeant Ransom's diary shows the horror with which he witnessed the ever increasing orgy of plunder and violence.

On May 25 he wrote: "Man killed by the raiders near where we slept. Head all pounded to pieces with a club. Murders an every day occurrence." On June 15: "Raiders now do just as they please, kill, plunder and steal in broad daylight, with no one to molest them." Two days later: "Saw a new comer pounded to a jelly by the raiders. His cries for relief were *awful*, but none came." On June 25: "Raiders kill some one now every day. No restraint in the least. Men who were no doubt respectable at home, are now the worse villains in the world." Two days later: "Raiders going on worse than ever before. A perfect pandemonium. Something must be done and that quickly. . . . It is hoped that the more peaceable sort will rise in their might and put them down."[7]

Some of the prisoners had already been trying to organize a force to cope with the murdering thieves but had failed. Men dreaded the approach of darkness, for though the Raiders did not hesitate to club, cut, stab, and rob during the daylight hours, they were much more active at night. John Northrop wrote in late June: "Not a night passes but the Camp is disturbed and cries of Murder are heard & some body is hurt & robbed." Ransom Chadwick commented: "the most horrible Barberism Amongst our owne men I ever red or hurd of wars than the Rebbs."[8]

Wednesday, June 29, was the day that marked the beginning of the end of the Raiders' reign of terror in the stockade. Conflicting accounts written long after the event and a dearth of on-the-spot reporting make it impossible to determine exactly what happened. Most descriptions of the Raiders' overthrow written in later years attribute their downfall to the efforts of an organization of fellow-inmates, but this explanation is clearly refuted by prisoners' diaries.[9] The generally indefinite character of diarists' statements indicates that most of them actually knew little of what occurred that eventful day. Doubtless many versions were bruited about. The following sketch, based on the most reliable sources available, seems to be correct in its essentials.

Somewhere around two o'clock in the afternoon a prisoner named Dowd manifested interest in a watch which two men were trying to sell, but he already had a watch; after examining the timepiece, he decided against purchasing a second one. The two men, who were robbers, thus learned that Dowd had both money and a watch. With two companions they soon returned and assaulted Dowd with clubs and brass knuckles as he sat trouserless in the shade of his "shebang." Encountering stouter resistance from Dowd than they had anticipated, the thieves withdrew. When Dowd went out in the street and put on his trousers, they set upon him with renewed vigor, overpowered him, seized his watch, and cut out the money which they found in his trousers' waistband.[10]

Dowd finally freed himself from his assailants and, with blood streaming from his badly cut face, hastened to the gate and reported his misfortune to a Confederate sergeant. Perceiving that Dowd was receiving a sympathetic hearing, other prisoners, including several sergeants of detachments, pressed forward to give particulars of the Raiders' depredations and to beg their keepers for protection. Captain Wirz came down to the gate to hear their plea, but so little perturbed were the Raiders that they actually committed one robbery while their fellow-prisoners denounced them and implored Wirz for help. The prison commander's ire was aroused. He promised, according to Northrop, that if the prisoners would point out the thieves "he would clear the Stockade of every son of a b—." Sergeant Forbes wrote: "Capt. Wurtz . . . came up with him [Dowd] and demanded that the robbers should be given up, under penalty of no rations for one week; in a short time a guard came in, and took eight men from a tent near the dead line on our side; very soon the camp was in an uproar, for the men came into the arrangement, and the raiders were hunted down from one end of the camp to the other; by dark the tumult was nearly over, but the raiders were not all caught yet; about 50 were taken outside; the issuing of rations was stopped."[11]

Prisoners directed guards to the dens of known Raiders, who, with a noticeable lack of the insolence they had so recently displayed, tried to conceal themselves. The guards seized the villains, taking out a few at a time and returning for more. When confronted by men armed with guns, the Raiders were meek, but they resisted vigorously when other prisoners attempted to take them in tow without assistance from the guards. One of the leaders swore he would not be taken alive. "He fought desperately," wrote Northrop, "but one of our men struck him from behind with a Stake fracturing his Skull and knocking him senseless. He was carried out the same as dead." According to Private Shatzel, "the Prisoners all formed a line on each side of the Road & the Rebs took the Raiders & let them run the Gauntlet & there was several of them killed for the Rebs gave every man a club & there was no light blows struck." Some of Sullivan's acquaintances observed him "marching under three bayonetts," and his guilty countenance moved one of them almost to pity. Nevertheless he was happy to see the culprit go and hoped that neither he nor any of his crew would be returned to the stockade.[12]

While some prisoners helped with the job of "clearing out the raiders," others ransacked their quarters for stolen property. The hunt yielded a large quantity of blankets, clothing, money, "watches, jewelry, and articles of all descriptions." According to Northrop, searchers found "two stockings filled with greenbacks, . . . one of watches, two gold, & other things." Others reported discovery of buried bodies and skeletons.[13] Raiders' tents were destroyed; tent poles, cooking utensils, and other items of value were confiscated. The crusade against the marauders and the search for loot continued the following day. Sergeant Ransom, too ill to leave his "shebang," wrote: "Little Terry, whom they could not find yesterday, was to-day taken. Had been hiding in an old well, or hole in the ground. Fought like a little tiger, but had to go." Among those "arrested" on Thursday were the four men who had robbed Dowd. They were "hustled to the gate . . . with a kick & a punch in the back & a swear & a shout from the crowd."[14]

Grateful prisoners shouted "Bully for the Captain," "bully for the guard." Commenting on suppression of the Raiders, Forbes wrote: "Captain Wurtz deserves great credit for his prompt action in the matter, and will probably be successful in checking the operations of these thieving scoundrels. . . . It is an act of justice on the part of the Confederate authorities which the men have not expected, they supposing that no notice would be taken of their complaints; but the reverse has been the case, and we can now feel secure from the attacks of daylight assassins or midnight murderers; the issuing of rations was promptly commenced as soon as the men known as ringleaders were captured."[15]

On June 30 General Winder issued General Order No. 57 authorizing establishment of a court by the prisoners for trial and punishment of the accused robbers and murderers. The order required that charges specify the time and place of alleged crimes, that copies of specifications be provided the accused, that testimony be taken as nearly as possible in the exact words of witnesses, and that all proceedings be kept in writing. Paragraph four provided that "The proceedings, findings, and sentence in each case will be sent to the commanding officer for record, and if found in order and proper, the sentence will be ordered for execution."[16]

With encouragement from prison authorities, inmates organized a police force called the "Regulators" to maintain order in the stockade. Captain Wirz had all sergeants of detachments assembled and twenty-four of them were selected as jurors. For each trial twelve jurymen were chosen by lot. Most of the suspects taken outside were returned to the stockade "on the ground that they had been decoyed & promises of good behavior." A few were sentenced to wear balls and chains; others were set in the stocks or strung up by the thumbs.[17] Sullivan, Collins, Delaney, Curtis, Sarsfield, and A. Munn—the last a member of the United States Navy— were found guilty of murder and sentenced to death by hanging.*

General Winder approved the executions and on Sunday evening, July 10, Father Whelan visited the condemned men in the stocks. Five of them were Catholics and received the consolations of their religion from the priest. Next morning prisoner-carpenters began construction of a scaffold near the

---

* Different sources give Munn's name as "Muir" (Northrop), "Muray" (Forbes), and Buer (Shatzel), but records of the United States Quartermaster General's office list him as "A. Munn, United States Navy." On Sullivan's headstone at Andersonville National Cemetery, appears the inscription: "W. Rickson, U.S.N." The quartermaster general's records indicate that his branch of service is unknown (John J. Flinn to Howard P. Bennett, August 1, 1957, letter in possession of the writer). But Daniel Buckley recorded his name as "Sulivan, state Not Known"; Shatzel wrote his name "Sulivan"; and Northrop knew him as "Cary Sullivan" when both were in the same company. Whatever his true name, he certainly was not known as "Rickson" in the stockade.

spot where rations were issued, several yards from the dead-line, eastward from the south gate. A group of Regulators, headed by a prisoner called "Limber Jim," formed a hollow square about the workers to keep the crowd from interfering and to avoid theft of the lumber, which was furnished by Wirz. Intense excitement gripped the stockade as preparations for the hanging neared completion. Some expected "that an attempt would be made, by the former associates of the doomed, to destroy the Scaffold & release them." Northrop described the scene: "Every passage for going to and fro thro' the prison was thronged almost to suffocation. Looking from my position near the Scaffold to the North side, . . . I beheld the most densely packed crowd I ever saw. The South side, if possible, was more densely thronged. They came from the extreme Northern and eastern parts until they could get no further." Another prisoner recalled years later that "All the hangers-on of the Rebel camp—clerks, teamsters, em-ployes, negros, [and] hundreds of white and colored women" gathered outside the stockade on a rise which commanded a good view of the scaffold.[18]

"The stockade," wrote Ransom, "was covered with rebels, who were fearful a break would be made" if the friends of the condemned Raiders attempted a rescue. "Artillery was pointed at us from all directions ready to blow us all into eternity in short order." About 4:30 P.M. the south gate opened and the six culprits were escorted into the stockade by Confederate guards, accompanied by Henry Wirz and Father Whelan. Turning them over to the Regulators, Wirz addressed the inmates in a short speech which Father Whelan later recalled as "something like this: 'Boys, I have taken these men out and now I return them to you, having taken good care of them. I now commit them to you. You can do with them as you see fit.' Then turning around to the con-demned men he said, 'May the Lord have mercy on your souls.' "[19]

Wirz then marched the guard out, and "Limber Jim" and his assistants started binding the hands of the doomed Raiders. "When Curtis was about to be bound," wrote Forbes, "he exclaimed, 'This cannot be,' and made a dash through the crowd and toward the creek." He reached the swamp, ran headlong into the boggy filth, and succeeded in getting across but was caught and dragged back. The condemned men asked Father Whelan to appeal to their fellow-prisoners to spare them. He did so, but his entreaty fell on deaf ears. Each was given a chance to make a final speech. Sullivan had nothing to say. Munn said he had been driven to crime by starvation and "evil companions." He professed to care nothing for his own life, "but the news that would be carried home to his people made him want to curse God he had ever been born."[20]

Collins denied that he had committed murder and begged that his life be spared for the sake of his wife and child. Curtis "said he didn't care a - - - -. Only hurry up and not be talking about it all day, making too much fuss over a very small matter." Delaney averred that he would rather hang than try to live on Andersonville rations. So long as he could steal, life in the stockade was tolerable; with that privilege removed, he preferred hanging. He said that Delaney was not his real name, that no one knew who he really was, therefore his friends would never know his fate, his Andersonville history dying with him. Sarsfield made the fanciest speech of all, giving a sort of life history of himself. He had begun his crimes by stealing food, and, like Munn, he blamed "evil associates" for bringing him to his end.[21]

When the speechmaking was concluded the executioners pulled a meal sack over the head of each doomed man and fixed the nooses while Father Whelan prayed aloud. About five o'clock the supports were jerked from under the platform and, in the words of Private Shatzel, "5 of them were launched into eternity without a struggle." Collins' rope broke and he fell to the ground. "But [wrote Shatzel] the rope was soon fixed & he was taken up the Seckond time then was the time he pleeded for mercy but it was to late & the platform was Jerked from under him & he left this world it was a terrible sight to witness but it had to be done."[22]

After hanging some fifteen minutes, the bodies were cut down, and the crowd dispersed quietly. Forbes wrote in his diary: "So ended the raid on Dowd, . . . And it is to be hoped that it will also end the system of organized robbery and ruffianism which has so long ruled this camp."[23] This hope was realized. "Limber Jim" and other prominent Regulators were detailed to outside work to remove them from danger of assassination by friends of the executed Raiders, but the Regulators did not disband. Although brawls and petty thefts continued, offenders were punished by the prison police force, which succeeded in maintaining a reasonable degree of order in the stockade after the hangings.

6

Danger and Dissension

WHEN GENERAL WINDER arrived at Andersonville, he was alarmed by the large number of prisoners held there and the fewness and poor discipline of the guards. On June 18, 1864, the day after he assumed command of the post, he wrote General Braxton Bragg, military advisor to President Davis, of the objectionable conditions at Camp Sumter. General Cobb, Commander of the Georgia Reserves, had sent four regiments, numbering two thousand men, to Andersonville, but sickness, details, and furloughs had drastically reduced their strength. With a total of 2,867 men, all but 371 of whom were reserves, Winder had only 1,462 present for duty and 23,120 prisoners on hand. He urged that his force be doubled.[1]

Next day General Winder saw Cobb at his headquarters in Macon and learned that the reserve commander could send him no more men at that time. Upon assuming command Winder had ordered the return of men absent from their regiments, but he doubted that this order would be obeyed. Measles and whooping cough were prevalent among his troops and more prisoners were arriving almost daily. The crowded condition of the stockade would be relieved by the addition to the prison which was then being made, but Winder considered his guard force "entirely inadequate" even if all were present and healthy. He wrote to Adjutant General Cooper of the serious shortage of provisions at Andersonville and warned that it was unsafe to hold so many prisoners at one place. He urged the establishment of another prison and suggested Union Springs in southeastern Alabama as a suitable site.[2]

Winder asked General Cobb to address President Davis on the subject of a new prison. Cobb wrote Davis that it was dangerous to send more prisoners to Andersonville and concurred in Winder's recommendation of Union Springs as a good location for another prison. Unquestionably it would be advisable, wrote Cobb, to strengthen the Andersonville guard, but it was impossible for him to supply more troops at the moment. With a thrust at Governor Brown, he informed the president that he was seriously handicapped by the fact that so many men had "been kept out of the Reserves by Gov. Brown's false certificate that they were necessary for the State Government."[3]

Meanwhile General Winder sought to remedy, insofar as possible, the lax discipline which prevailed in the reserve regiments. He ordered commanding officers "to establish their camps and regulate their guard in accordance with Army Regulations." Calling the attention of all officers to the duties of guards and sentinels, he informed them that they would be held accountable for escapes and all difficulties "arising from the failure of an intelligent and rigid performance of duty on the part of troops acting under their commands." He ordered a thorough daily policing of all guard camps, required officers to quarter themselves with their commands, prohibited their leaving camp limits "without the knowledge and consent of their immediate superior officer," and directed that at least one commissioned officer should be on duty with each company at all times. The general further directed that troops were not to absent themselves from camp without an officer's permission, that they should never be more than a mile away, and that under no circumstances was any company to permit the absence of more than five men. He strictly prohibited "all persons" from trading with prisoners. Violators, if citizens, were to "have their articles seized and confiscated"; if soldiers, they were to "be promptly and severely punished."

Winder was especially concerned about prisoners escaping and the possibility of an outbreak. Writing to Cooper on June 22 of the "fearful responsibility" placed upon him, he expressed hope that the government had enough confidence in him to give him what he required for proper performance of his duties. "We have this morning," he wrote, "24,193 prisoners of war . . . and only 1,178 reserves (as raw as troops can be) for guard for all purposes." He cited as evidence of the need of increased vigilance the fact that he had just found under the stockade a tunnel fourteen feet deep and almost one hundred feet long. Maintaining that "the breaking out of these prisoners would be more disastrous than a defeat for the army," Winder begged that at least two thousand additional troops be sent him. He feared that his effective force would be indefinitely reduced by measles and whooping cough. The general's letter was submitted to Secretary of War Seddon, who agreed that the guard force was "alarmingly small," but he could do no more than instruct Cooper to investigate the possibility of getting more reserves from Cobb.[4]

Deeming the state of affairs at his post critical and fretting over irregular mail deliveries, Winder, on June 24, sent one of his assistants, Lieutenant Samuel Boyer Davis, to Richmond with a letter describing to Cooper the situation at Andersonville. Extensiveness of recently discovered tunnels indicated that the prisoners had been brought to the point of desperation by conditions in the stockade. One underground passage extended 130 feet beyond the palisades. The general also stated that he had evidence that a Federal agent sent by General Sherman had been communicating with the prisoners prior to his arrival at the post. Winder was particularly alarmed by the conviction that a portion of the citizenry in the vicinity of Andersonville was disloyal to the Confederacy and actively sympathetic to the stockade inmates.

Convinced that some of these disaffected persons were in communication with the prisoners, General Winder believed they should "be looked after." He requested Cooper to send some Richmond detectives to assist him in watching and counteracting the baneful influence of Union sympathizers. Emphasizing the "great responsibility" of his command, "the rawness of the troops," and "the great danger of a successful outbreak among the prisoners," he predicted that such a disaster would bring devastation and total ruin to southwestern Georgia. "Every house," he wrote, "would be burned, violence to women [would result, as well as] destruction of crops, carrying off negroes, horses, mules, and wagons."[5]

Two weeks later Winder again wrote Adjutant General Cooper to inquire if Lieutenant Davis had arrived in Richmond and to repeat his appeal for aid. By this time the general seems to have reached a condition bordering on hysteria. "There is treason going on all around us," he wrote, "even to depositing arms in the adjacent counties to arm the prisoners." Complaining that he was forced to rely on incompetent investigators, he reiterated his plea for detectives. The reserves he described as "raw and dissatisfied." Twelve of them, he reported, had deserted the previous night. They could not be depended upon in case of an emergency.

The same day, July 9, Winder wrote General Cobb: "Matters have arrived at that point *when I must* have reinforcements." Informing Cobb of the "great dissatisfaction among the Reserves," he stated his conviction that they were determined to abandon the prison and added that he was powerless to stop them. He continued: "Now, General, it is morally certain that if the Government or the people of Georgia don't come to my relief and that instantly I cannot hold these prisoners and they must submit to see Georgia devastated, by *the prisoners.*" He inquired if Cobb could raise a volunteer force to come to his aid immediately, adding: "Twenty four hours may be too late."[6]

Sending troops was out of the question, but the urgency of Winder's appeal induced Cobb to go to Andersonville in person. He found everything quiet and decided that General Winder had exaggerated his difficulties. Cobb wrote his wife on July 11 that many of the reserves were unhappy about not getting leave and were threatening desertion in an attempt to frighten Winder into granting more furloughs. He spent a day at the prison and gave the guards a thirty-minute talk in the sun to boost their morale. When he left, he thought both officers and men were "perfectly content and satisfied."

On July 6 Assistant Adjutant General Hugh L. Clay wrote General Winder that if his guard force were insufficient, he should ask Cobb for more reserves, since troops could be drawn from no other source. Clay stated that Winder had been "requested some time since to select a place in Alabama" to which some of the Andersonville prisoners could be sent and urged him to remove as many as he thought expedient as soon as he could decide on the location. Two days later General Cobb wrote Winder that it was impossible for him to increase the Andersonville guard at that time and suggested that Winder push the project for a new prison in Alabama. "I certainly should not wait," wrote Cobb, "for any further orders or authority from Richmond, but at once press, with all expedition the work."[7]

After an absence of almost a month, Lieutenant Davis returned from Richmond with what Winder considered "a very severe censure" from Adjutant General Cooper. Defending himself against this censure, General Winder reported that his command at Andersonville as of July 20 aggregated only 2,421 officers and men, of whom 517 were sick. Duties other than guarding prisoners required 227 men daily and the artillery company numbered 126, leaving only 1,551 for guard duty. The daily guard requirement was 613. This included 166 stockade sentinels, 73 hospital guards, 206 pickets around the stockade, 43 railroad-bridge guards and outlying pickets, and 125 guards for the woodcutting detail and other work parties. Cooper had suggested "placing the prisoners properly." Winder professed to be puzzled as to his meaning. "I know of but one way to place them," he wrote, "and that is to put them into the stockade, where they have between four and five square yards to the man." This included the uninhabitable borders of the stream.[8]

While the post commander fretted over the paucity and incompetency of guards and the danger of revolt among the prisoners, prison administration was hampered by deficiencies of all sorts. Winder was compelled to send an officer to Columbia, South Carolina, in search of books in which to keep prison records. He telegraphed Richmond to request the tents which prisoners had occupied at Belle Isle for use in the prison hospital. Post quartermaster Dick Winder sent out desperate appeals for mules, horses, and wagons. "I cannot get along without . . . transportation," he wrote the chief inspector of field transportation in Augusta, "and you must either furnish me or give me authority to impress." General Cobb with much difficulty obtained a number of wagons and teams for his reserves and sent three of them to Andersonville. A squabble ensued between reserve regimental commanders, who wished the teams to be used only by reserves, and General Winder, who issued an order turning them over to the post quartermaster. Cobb tried to smooth matters over. He wrote General Winder that the transportation facilities were to be used "as in your judgment is best for the public service." Winder was to "order and direct their use, as you may see proper." But Cobb wanted them "to remain subject to my control" and asked that the order turning them over to Captain Winder be modified.[9]

Shortage of provisions also troubled General Winder. On July 25 he wrote General Cooper: "There are 29,400 prisoners, 2,650 troops, 500 negroes and other laborers and not a ration at the post." He thought the situation dangerous. Though he had directed that rations for at least ten days be kept on hand, this order had never been enforced. Cooper submitted Winder's letter to Commissary General Lucius B. Northrop, who informed Cooper that Winder had nothing to do with feeding prisoners—that this was the concern of the commissary general. The factious Northrop contended that if General Winder thought the prisoners likely to rebel because of short rations or that anything in connection with supplies was not as it should be, it was "his duty to report his views to the Commissary-General." Asserting that Winder had "no right to give any orders on the subject," Northrop continued: "Had General Winder's orders for ten days' rations for over 32,000 men to be kept ahead been complied with, I should have countermanded it. . . . General Winder thinks the prisoners should have ten days' ahead, while the army may be restricted in a day's ration.

"If General Winder thinks that the subsistence of the prisoners has been or is critical, and he is anxious about their remaining quiet or in good condition, he can communicate with the Commissary-General on the subject if he pleases, and he will bring to his mind appropriate considerations which may satisfy his anxiety about them, or if he prefers to communicate with the Quartermaster-General, who is responsible for their custody, the latter will receive from the Commissary-General such information which will satisfy him that the prisoners will be duly cared for and not suffer until the army is pinched."[10]

As a matter of fact the prisoners were then suffering for food and other essentials. Dick Winder was unable to obtain sufficient funds either for paying troops or for purchasing supplies for prisoners. Lack of space prevented improvements within the stockade and essential work was blocked by want of lime, lumber, axes, wheelbarrows, iron, sheet-iron, and other tools and supplies. Wirz reported on August 1: "vinegar and soap, both very important articles, are very seldom issued, as the commissary says he cannot get them."

Despite General Winder's concern for the security of the prison, some citizens in the neighborhood thought him careless in the paroling of prisoners. One of these residents wrote Governor Brown complaining of some three hundred unguarded, unsupervised parolees outside the stockade, talking and trading with Confederate soldiers, going about in the country, buying vegetables, getting information on Confederate supplies and troop movements, and constituting a danger to the community. Some of them were employed in cutting logs for the addition to the stockade, some in burying the dead. Others worked as carpenters, cooks, bakers, teamsters, or litter-bearers. The unnamed letter-writer, described by Brown as "one whose judgment and veracity may well be trusted," thought it probable that by cooperating with the prisoners in the stockade, they could engineer a successful escape of the whole body of prisoners. Governor Brown sent this letter to Secretary of War Seddon, who asked Adjutant General Cooper to refer it to General Winder with a request for a report of the facts. Winder's report convinced Seddon that he had "been obliged to grant the paroles and employ the prisoners" as he had done, but the secretary urged the exercise of "great caution to obviate the danger that may result from these men being at large."[11]

As the Union forces under General Sherman continued to advance on Atlanta, Winder grew increasingly uneasy about the possibility of a Federal cavalry raid on Andersonville. Following the engagement at Kenesaw Mountain (June 27), General Joseph E. Johnston, in command of the Army of Tennessee opposing Sherman's forces, withdrew to the east side of the Chattahoochee River. On July 8 General Cobb wrote Winder that although a Federal movement in the direction of Andersonville did not seem imminent, they should make all possible preparation for that eventuality. Three days later Johnston telegraphed President Davis: "I strongly recommend the distribution of the U.S. prisoners now at Andersonville immediately." Davis replied that Johnston had all the troops available for guarding or distributing prisoners and must advise Winder regarding the proper disposition of captives.[12]

On July 10 Sherman dispatched one of his cavalry commanders, General Lovell H. Rousseau, from Decatur, Alabama, with a force of twenty-five hundred men to strike a blow at the West Point and Montgomery Railroad between Tuskegee and Opelika, just across the Chattahoochee from Columbus, Georgia. Rousseau's orders were to wreck the railroad, burn the station buildings at Opelika, and if he encountered no serious opposition, make a threatening gesture toward Columbus before turning northward up the Chattahoochee to join Sherman between Atlanta and Marietta, "doing all the mischief possible" en route. On the seventeenth, eighteenth, and nineteenth the Federal cavalry destroyed over thirty miles of track between Opelika and Chehaw Station, a number of bridges, the water tank at Notasulga, and the railroad stations at Notasulga, Loachapoka, Auburn, and Opelika.[13]

Rousseau's raid frightened the residents of southwestern Georgia. Reports coming in to Cobb and Winder warned that rescue of Federal prisoners might be the raiders' objective. Confederate General Samuel ("Sad Sam") Jones, commanding the Department of South Carolina, Georgia, and Florida, telegraphed Cobb on the eighteenth that the commander at Columbus had reported Federal cavalry advancing on Andersonville. Cobb was to send reserves to protect the prison. Governor Brown had called on all able-bodied men to come to the defense of Atlanta. Forwarding to Winder a telegram from Columbus announcing that city threatened, Cobb advised him to inform Confederate exempts and details in the vicinity that they were not expected to respond to Governor Brown's call and that Winder was authorized to summon them to his support in case of attack. "Keep them subject to your order," wrote Cobb. While he doubted that an attack on Andersonville was intended, he thought it best to keep Winder informed of military developments. Seeking to steady the excitable Camp Sumter commander, Cobb assured him that a regiment of dismounted Confederate cavalry proceeding from Fort Valley toward the Georgia-Alabama border was "instructed to have regard to the defense of Andersonville as well as Columbus."[14]

Unaware that Johnston had been replaced on the seventeenth by General John B. Hood, Cobb wrote him on July 18 for assistance in preventing militiamen home on furlough and others not subject to military duty under laws of the Confederacy from leaving endangered areas. Andersonville's small force needed reinforcements, but to remove any of Cobb's reserves would weaken vital points. He admitted the wisdom of calling to the front those men serving in less important capacities but argued that compliance with Brown's call in southwestern Georgia would "take away all means of reinforcing the threatened points." Further, the production of agricultural products was essential and, more serious, the Negro population required a police force. Assuming that Johnston and Brown were on good terms, Cobb begged the general to use his influence with the governor to forestall the removal of any more men from the region about Macon and Andersonville.

As soon as Winder heard of Federal raiders in eastern Alabama, he frantically ordered construction of fortifications about his post. The prisoners got wind of what was going on and became hopeful of being rescued. One of them noted in his diary on the twenty-first: "it is reported that our Cavalry is advancing on this place & the Rebs have got some 500 negroes to work throwing up earth works they are to work night & day & from the looks they are afraid of something besides the Prisoners." Two days later he wrote: "the Rebs are at work on their Fortifycations yet night & day they appear to be in a hell of a hurrey for some cause or another."[15]

The day after he took command of the Army of Tennessee, Hood inquired whether or not Cobb was able to secure his prisoners. "If Andersonville is seriously threatened," he telegraphed, "& there is danger of release of prisoners I

will send reinforcements." He returned to Cobb five hundred
southwestern Georgia militiamen, who arrived at Macon on
the twenty-first. Cobb sent them on to General Winder with
the suggestion that those not needed be sent home to police
Negroes and furnish corn for the army. While these troops
were en route to Macon, Hood fought the losing Battle of
Peachtree Creek and the day after their arrival suffered another reverse in the Battle of Atlanta. He asked Cobb to
return the soldiers. Requesting "every man to be sent forward
that can bear an arm," he urged that unless Andersonville
were immediately threatened only the regular garrison be
left there. Cobb replied that he would forward Hood's request to Winder but alleged that the men were sorely needed
to make Andersonville secure, to supply corn and other provisions for the Confederacy, and to control the Negro population, the condition of which had "already created the
greatest excitement and alarm" throughout southwestern
Georgia.[16]

The reserve commander's pleas availed nothing. The governor telegraphed him that Hood had said all militiamen,
including those detained at Andersonville, must go to Atlanta. Therefore, Brown declared, he must "direct them to
go forward." Cobb forwarded copies of the correspondence
between himself and Hood and Brown to Winder, writing:
"The militia now with you are ordered to the front. I have
no troops to send in their place."[17]

Meanwhile the raider scare had reached Richmond. Learning that five hundred Federal prisoners had left Charlotte,
North Carolina, for Andersonville on July 23, Secretary of
War Seddon ordered that no more prisoners be sent there
for the present. This order was referred to General William
M. Gardner who had replaced General Winder as chief
custodian of prisoners in the vicinity of the Confederate capital. Gardner complained that the vagueness of his appointment left him in doubt as to where his jurisdiction ended
and that of Winder began. At any rate, there was no other
prison to which enlisted men could be sent.[18]

A real threat to Andersonville came from Stoneman's raid,
which began July 27. General George Stoneman, commanding five thousand cavalry, was ordered by General Sherman

to a point near Lovejoy's Station where he was to meet another cavalry force and destroy the railroad between Macon and Atlanta. Stoneman asked Sherman to permit him, after carrying out his orders, to "proceed to Macon & Andersonville and release our prisoners of war confined at those points." Captivated by the idea, Sherman consented. The sight of Union cavalry moving toward McDonough brought the result that General Cobb's arguments had failed to produce. On the twenty-eighth he received instructions that the militia should remain at Andersonville "for the present."[19]

The same day that Stoneman left Atlanta General Winder issued *An appeal to the citizens of Macon, Randolph, Schley, Terrell, Baker, Calhoun, Lee, Sumter, and Dougherty Counties* for "2,000 negroes, properly supplied with axes, spades, and picks, and supported by the requisite number of wagons and teams" to complete the fortification of Camp Sumter. Asserting that the safety of the people of these counties and the interests of the government demanded immediate action, he expressed a desire to avoid exercise of his authority to impress, and promised: "Whether the works are completed or not the negroes shall be returned to secure fodder, &c." The response to this appeal was less enthusiastic than Winder would have liked, but prisoners noted an augmentation of the work force as well as an increased concern for the internal security of the prison.[20]

As Stoneman's raiders rode southward General Winder sent out fervent entreaties for news of their whereabouts and strength. On July 30, two miles east of Macon, a force of "Georgia reserves, citizens, local companies, and the militia," led by General Cobb, repulsed Stoneman and a detachment estimated by Cobb as numbering twenty-eight hundred. Next day General Alfred Iverson's cavalry routed the main body at Hillsborough near Clinton, capturing General Stoneman and about five hundred others.[21]

The defeat of Stoneman did not end Yankee raiding south of Atlanta, and concern for southwestern Georgia did not abate. Work on the Andersonville defenses continued. For purposes of both offense and defense the labor force set up a second line of palisades around the main stockade at a distance of about ninety feet. A third stockade line around the other two, designed to provide a covered way for marching troops between forts, was commenced but never finished.[22]

General Winder intensified his efforts to get the prisoners moved. Learning that the Federal officers were to be removed from Macon, he suggested sending some of the Andersonville prisoners there. Cobb objected that this would be "bad policy" for various reasons, among them the fact that it would invite Federal raids on Macon which was "almost defenceless." After Rousseau's raid the idea of locating a prison in eastern Alabama was abandoned, and in early August Captains W. Sidney Winder and D. W. Vowles chose a prison site five miles from Millen in east central Georgia. Cobb protested to Secretary of War Seddon that new prisons should be established in different states. This would permit use of state reserves as guards, he reasoned; but reserves could be used only in their home states, and the result of having several prisons in one state would be the necessity of obtaining guards from the army.[23]

But Winder did not like using reserves. He asked Cobb to trade him militia for his reserves. Cobb replied that only the War Department had power to remove the reserves from Andersonville. He assured Winder that he would be happy to take his reserves to the front if he could but reminded him of the militia's limited time of service and of the fact that Joe Brown could send them home at any time he chose. Instead of getting rid of the reserves, Winder lost what militia he had. In mid-August Hood asked for the militia at Andersonville and promised to send organized troops as replacements. Winder was slow to comply with his request. He tried to dispose of some reserves by sending them to Macon when no orders for their movement had been issued, but Cobb returned them and made his disapprobation clear to Winder. Hood finally got the militia and on September 6 ordered Cobb to send all the reserves at Macon to Andersonville.[24]

Relations between Generals Cobb and Winder, which seem to have been pleasant enough in the beginning, became increasingly strained. Winder's antipathy for the reserves made it impossible for him to esteem their commander, and Cobb developed a distinct dislike for Winder. To the War Department Winder made "grave complaint of the disorderly conduct and plunder of the Reserves," especially the officers. Apprised of these complaints, Cobb expressed his surprise, writing Winder that since he had made no mention of the matter to him, he was unprepared for such news. He was responsible for the conduct of officers in his command, Cobb continued, but unless he knew of these evils, he saw no way to correct them. He claimed it his special duty to investigate Winder's charges, punish the guilty, and take steps to avoid repetitions. Cobb invited Winder to name the offending officers and prefer charges against them so that they could be punished according to regulations, adding that he should have followed that procedure in the beginning.[25]

Lamenting that the reserves were "the most ungovernable set I ever had anything to do with," Winder expressed to Adjutant General Cooper his desire to exchange them for other troops and asked that the commanding officer of the reserves at Andersonville, Brigadier General Lucius J. Gartrell, be relieved. Apprised of this request, Cobb wrote Cooper that it was to be expected, "for he [Winder] expressed his regret that Genl. Gartrell should be assigned to that command, before he ever entered upon the duties of it, and he has been increasing in his efforts to get clear of him. If Genl. Gartrell had been the equal in every respect of Genl. R. E. Lee, I have no doubt the same complaints would have been made—for Genl. Winder was determined in advance not to be satisfied with the arrangement."

Explaining to Cooper why, in his opinion, Winder was "so quarrelous in reference both to the Reserves and Genl. Gartrell," Cobb wrote: "there is a mutual dislike between him and these troops and each party is conscious of the existence of that feeling on the part of the others." Advising Cooper that Winder had made no response to repeated requests for charges and specifications against intractable reserve officers and men, he continued: "he is not more anxious to get rid of the Reserves than I am to get rid of his complaints against them, and it will therefore be most acceptable and agreeable to me to have any arrangement made by which the Reserves shall no longer be in any way connected with the General and his prisons."[26]

Of course Winder was not the only one who rated the

reserves as poor soldiers. Colonel Daniel T. Chandler inspected Andersonville in early August,[27] and he wrote: "These
troops are entirely without discipline, and their officers are
incapable of instructing them, being ignorant of their own
duties." But the 230 regular troops then at Andersonville, a
detachment of the Fifty-fifth Georgia, were worse.* Of them
Chandler reported: "They are thoroughly demoralized, muti-
nous, and entirely without discipline. . . . The colonel of this
regiment, C. B. Harkie, though armed at the time, permitted
his men to drag him from a railroad car and march him up
and down the platform of the depot, and to take him from
his tent, place him on a stump, and compel him to go through
the manual of arms with a tent-pole, and to sign and forward
his resignation to the War Department. This last he recalled
by a telegram. . . . He had recently rejoined the command,
but dares not assume command of the regiment."

In addition to these boisterous regulars and the First, Second, Third, and Fourth Regiments of the Georgia Reserves,
the Andersonville guard of August 5 included a company of
Florida light artillery and a battalion of Georgia militia. The
four reserve regiments totaled 3,067 officers and men, the
artillery company numbered 162, and the militia battalion,
516. Of the 3,975 troops attached to the post, 647 were on
sick report, 385 absent without leave, 227 on leave, 212 on
special duty, 185 on detached service, and 48 under arrest,
leaving only 2,282 effective for duty.† In addition to frequent
details, 784 men were required for daily duty, and Chandler
considered the strength at least one thousand men short of
what was needed to give the men proper rest. He characterized the artillery company as "an efficient body of men, well
drilled, disciplined, and officered." They had sixteen pieces of
field artillery, some in position, others awaiting completion of
the works. All the militia and many of the reserves were
without bayonets; 452 of the entire force had no arms of
any kind.

* This detachment consisted of men who were absent from their command
when the Fifty-fifth Georgia was captured at Cumberland Gap.
† Failure of these figures to balance is explained by the fact that a few
men were reported both as under arrest and as absent without leave, and
others as both sick and on leave. See *O.R.,* Ser. 2, VII, 552.

Colonel Chandler's inspection of Andersonville was the result of a desire on the part of Richmond authorities to improve the health and comfort of the prisoners, the security and administration of the prison, and management of the hospitals for prisoners and guards, or, if expedient, to move the prison to another locality. Adjutant General Cooper instructed him to "make a careful and minute inspection of the prison" with these points in mind, report his findings, and make such recommendations as seemed advisable. Chandler reported the wretched conditions in the stockade: the congestion, the polluted stream and filthy swamp, lack of shelter, unsystematic arrangement of hovels, grossly inadequate medical care and shocking mortality rate, short, defective rations, insufficient cooking utensils and fuel, scarcity of soap and clothing, and complete absence of police and sanitary regulations. The dead received callous treatment, he noted, "their hands in many instances being . . . mutilated with an ax in the removal of . . . rings." The hospital accommodations he found "totally insufficient," and many of the medical officers "very inefficient."

The colonel could see no advantage in moving the prison. He considered its location as healthy and as inaccessible to enemy raids as any in the state, and removal would not reduce the cost of subsistence or increase the prisoners' comfort. He recommended that no more prisoners be sent to Andersonville and that the number there be reduced to fifteen thousand by sending two thousand to Macon immediately, the remainder of the excess to be sent to a new prison site in southwestern Alabama and to Camp Lawton, the prison under construction near Millen. He submitted a plan for draining the prison grounds and urged its execution. Chandler suggested that clothing and soap be issued to the prisoners; that prison regulations be posted inside the stockade; that the post quartermaster be authorized to impress wagons, teams, and sawmills; that bakepans be furnished for the prison bakery; and that a telegraph line be constructed between Fort Valley and Andersonville.

This inspecting officer was outraged by what he observed at Andersonville, but for some of the personnel he had words of approbation. Most of the staff officers, he reported, were

"intelligent and efficient in the discharge of their duties."
Chandler described quartermaster Dick Winder as "energetic
and efficient," and Colonel Henry Forno, commander of the
guard forces, as "active, intelligent, energetic, and zealous."
Of the commander of the interior of the prison he wrote:
"Capt. Henry Wirz . . . is entitled to commendation for his
untiring energy and devotion to the discharge of the multi-
farious duties of his position, for which he is preeminently
qualified." Concurring in a recommendation which General
Winder had made for Wirz's promotion, Chandler further
recommended that he be given at least three assistants, "especially selected for their fitness for the position."

Others Colonel Chandler rated less highly. Captain J. W.
Armstrong, assistant commissary of subsistence, he adjudged
"a very inefficient officer and entirely incompetent for the
discharge of the duties of his position." He recommended
Armstrong's immediate removal. Captain Samuel T. Bailey,
assistant adjutant general, he pronounced "mentally and physically incapacitated" for the performance of his duties. Chandler also noted that the chief surgeon had represented one
surgeon and two assistant surgeons "as being incompetent and
inefficient." But the part of Chandler's report which did most
to make it a subject of controversy ever since was the following sentence: "My duty requires me respectfully to recommend a change in the officer in command of the post, Brig.
Gen. J. H. Winder, and the substitution in his place of some
one who unites both energy and good judgment with some
feelings of humanity and consideration for the welfare and
comfort (so far as is consistent with their safe-keeping) of
the vast number of unfortunates placed under his control;
some one who at least will not advocate deliberately and in
cold blood the propriety of leaving them in their present condition until their number has been sufficiently reduced by death
to make the present arrangements suffice for their accommodation, and who will not consider it a matter of self-laudation
and boasting that he has never been inside the stockade, a
place the horrors of which it is difficult to describe, and which
is a disgrace to civilization; the condition of which he might
by the exercise of a little energy and judgment, even with the
limited means at his command, have considerably improved."

After examining this report, Colonel Robert H. Chilton, assistant adjutant and inspector general, concurred by order of General Cooper in Chandler's recommendations and submitted them to the Secretary of War with the comment: "The condition of the prison at Andersonville is a reproach to us as a nation." A War Department clerk's digest of the report stated: "the frightful per centum of mortality . . . appears to be only a necessary consequence of the criminal indifference of the authorities charged with their [the prisoners'] care and custody." Colonel Chilton ordered the chief of the Engineer Bureau, General Jeremy F. Gilmer, to put into effect the plan for drainage of the prison grounds and reclamation of the swamp; he directed General Winder to have the Fifty-fifth Georgia brought under proper discipline, court-martial Colonel Harkie, correct the deficiencies in "proper attention, provisions, medicines, and accommodations," and report the action taken in compliance with these orders.[28]

Winder asked his subordinates to prepare answers to the portions of Chandler's report which related to their departments. Three officers reported that the supply of wood in the stockade was abundant. Surgeon White confessed that medical care was insufficient, but pleaded: "Ten times the number of medical officers at present on duty at the prison would be inadequate." Wirz admitted deficiencies in cooking and baking facilities but stated that it had been impossible to obtain the materials necessary to overcome this difficulty. Major F. W. Dillard, the Columbus quartermaster, he reported, had answered a request for sheet-iron for bakepans with the remark that it "should be used for our army, and not for the Yankees."

Wirz had tried, he alleged, to act as Colonel Chandler's guide and explain matters to him, but the inspecting officer had been more interested in hearing what prisoners had to say. "I saw very soon," wrote Wirz, "that he would be made the plaything of cute Yankees, who would give him most horrible descriptions of their sufferings, . . . owing doubtlessly to the sympathy which his looks indicated he had for them." Captain Wirz credited Chandler with the remark: "This beats anything I ever saw; it is, indeed, a hell on earth," but added that Chandler's assistant, Major W. Carvel Hall, rated Andersonville "about on a par with the Federal prison at Johnson's Island, which is represented as being the best prison in the North."

Forwarding these reports to the Adjutant and Inspector General's Office, General Winder contended that Chandler's inspection had been "very superficial," that his sympathy "for the prisoners was so apparent that it attracted the attention of both officers and citizens, and was the subject of very general remark," and that his determination "to report unfavorably of everything he saw or heard" was obvious. Winder claimed to have information from two different sources that Colonel Chandler had, prior to his arrival at Andersonville, told various "gentlemen and ladies" that the prisoners had been cruelly treated and informed them "what his report would be." In fact, Winder had, so he asserted, after conversing briefly with Chandler upon his arrival at the post, "before he could have seen anything, . . . told the officers that he had determined to report unfavorably and would not see things in their true light." As an example of Chandler's biased reporting, Winder cited his account of Colonel Harkie's treatment at the hands of his men, given as if the incidents occurred at Andersonville when, according to Winder, they took place "if at all" over a year previously at Cumberland Gap. While confessing that one "transaction . . . really did take place at this post . . . upon which charges might have been framed" against Harkie, Winder observed that Chandler had not mentioned it and stated that he could not comply with the order to have Harkie court-martialed because Chandler had not specified time, place, and witnesses.

In short, Winder branded Chandler's charges "not true." Colonel Chilton referred Winder's reply to Chandler with a request that he furnish full and clear explanations of all points in his report which had been challenged by Winder and his officers. Major W. Carvel Hall flatly denied Wirz's statement that he had equated Andersonville with Johnson's Island. On the contrary, Chandler had consulted with him in preparing the report, Hall declared, and added: "I fully concur in it."[29]

Some historians, accusing Chandler of "animus toward

. . . Winder," have maintained that his report was "wholly unfair to the prison administration."[30] It is true, as William B. Hesseltine has pointed out, that Chandler, according to his own statement written in May, 1865, was a Union sympathizer at the time he inspected Andersonville Prison. Having resigned his commission in the United States Army in December, 1862, Chandler was arrested the following February while attempting to cross the Potomac River into Virginia to conduct business transactions. After almost nine months' imprisonment, he was eventually exchanged for a nephew of Andrew Johnson. He remained in Richmond until February, 1864, when he accepted an appointment in the Confederate Adjutant General's Department with the rank of lieutenant colonel. Although Chandler apparently felt his acceptance warranted by the fact that he was "at the time held liable to conscription," he affirmed when seeking Federal amnesty at the close of the war that he soon came to consider the action as "the one great error" of his life and determined to seize the first opportunity of honorably resuming his allegiance to the Union.[31]

But to conclude from these facts that Chandler misrepresented conditions at Andersonville is questionable. It leaves unexplained Major Hall's unhesitating and emphatic backing of Chandler. More significant perhaps are the comments which Colonel Chilton made after studying General Winder's response to the report and Chandler's answer to Winder's allegations of prejudice and falsehood. The reports of Winder and his subordinate officers were prepared for the purpose of refuting Chandler, but Chilton advised Secretary of War Seddon

in no instance is a single statement satisfactorily controverted; on the contrary, they are sustained, and the subsequent report, called for by this office, of Colonel Chandler clearly explains anything that may have been indefinitely expressed and completely establishes the truthfulness of his statements. . . . extracts [from Chandler's report] were referred to General Winder . . . with specific instructions and were returned without compliance with those instructions, but with mere attempts at denial; . . . the replies, although intended to

contradict and oppose the statements, sustain them. . . .
in characterizing the statements "as false" he [Winder]
imputes to Colonel Chandler "conduct unbecoming an
officer and a gentleman" upon no evidence to sustain the
assertion and without any warrant or necessity for the
language.
    . . . it is respectfully recommended that such action
may be ordered as will . . . rebuke an officer who seems
to be as careless and indifferent respecting the honor of
another's reputation as he is reported to be to the dictates of humanity.[32]

It may be true that Colonel Chandler went to Andersonville resolved to make an unfavorable report, but proof of
prejudiced motivation for a statement is not proof that the
statement is false. The fact is that if Chandler wished to
depict the prison as a noxious place, he could do so without
deviating one whit from absolute truth. One may disagree
with his recommendations or his evaluation of officers at the
post, but prison conditions involved facts rather than opinions; and Chandler's description is supported by prisoners'
diaries, by reports of other inspectors, and by reports of
Winder, Wirz, Chief Surgeon White, and others responsible
for prison administration. Winder's protest that the Fifty-
fifth Georgia's abuse of Colonel Harkie did not occur at
Andersonville could not gloss over the more important facts
that the regiment was undisciplined and that Harkie was poor
officer material—facts which Winder did not deny. His other
objections to Chandler's statements were similar evasions of
the fundamental points—namely that conditions at Andersonville were deplorable and that possibilities of improving them
had not been exhausted.

General Winder's reaction to Chandler's report challenged
the colonel's honesty, and the question became an issue of
veracity between the two, although Colonel Chilton indicated
no doubt as to who was misrepresenting the case. Expressing
an urgent desire to have the matter investigated, Chandler
requested a court of inquiry, but the War Department felt
unable to spare officers of appropriate rank; and although he
chafed under Winder's imputations and repeatedly implored
the War Department for some action in the case, none was

ever taken. Chandler gave up his pursuit of a settlement only when Winder died in February, 1865.[33]

A few days after Colonel Chandler's inspection, the same heavy rains that opened up "Providence Spring" swelled Stockade Creek to four or five feet above its normal level and washed away portions of the wall on the east and west sides of the stockade. Order was maintained in the prison by the Regulators, aided by the sixteen artillery pieces trained on the inmates. No escape was attempted, but General Winder, on the verge of panic, telegraphed Richmond that whether the stockade could be saved was doubtful and begged that facilities be sent to Millen to hasten completion of the prison there. He kept the troops under arms for about sixty hours while the damage was repaired, and afterward he wrote Adjutant General Cooper: "Never in my life have I spent so anxious a time. If we had not had a large negro force working on the defenses I think it would have been impossible to have saved the place."[34]

Belatedly Dick Winder set about moving the cookhouse from the stream flowing through the prison, and immediately following Chandler's departure from Andersonville prisoners were put to work carrying lumber into the stockade for construction of barracks. These projects were impeded by the same conditions that thwarted so many others — want of funds, tools, and equipment. Ten days after work on the barracks commenced Captain Winder wrote the Columbus quartermaster that work had almost ceased for lack of nails. In addition to two hundred kegs of nails, he requested "a shipment of iron and steel," 250 tents, a pair of bellows for the blacksmith shop, and twenty-five iron kettles of forty- to sixty-gallon capacity for cooking. Two weeks later the quartermaster was desperately trying to get a quarter of a million dollars to pay the outstanding debts of his office.[35]

Despite the obstacles involved, the new cookhouse was eventually completed, and by September 1 the frames of four barracks, each capable of housing 270 men, had been erected along the north end of the stockade with two more near completion. A week later prisoners were moving in. But when General Sherman occupied Atlanta on September 2, Confederate authorities decided that it was no longer safe to hold captives at Andersonville and ordered removal of all those able to be transported. On September 7 the first eighteen detachments left for Charleston and Florence, South Carolina. The following day prisoners who had occupied barracks were ordered out to make room for those who were too sick to be moved.[36]

7

Medical Care

THE CHIEF CAUSE of high mortality at Andersonville was the character of the care and treatment provided for the sick. When the hospital was moved outside the prison in the latter part of May, it was relocated near the southeast corner of the stockade on a plat of something less than two acres. Rapid increase in the number of patients compelled frequent expansion until it covered about five acres. A small, sluggish stream flowed across the southern part of the grounds and united with Stockade Creek a short distance to the west. Large trees afforded welcome shade.

Aside from these shade trees the only shelter was an inadequate supply of tents. Less than a month after the new hospital site was occupied, Chief Surgeon Isaiah H. White reported that he had only 209 small tents, poorly adapted to hospital use. Whereas no more than 800 patients could be comfortably accommodated, 1,020 seriously sick were crowded into these deficient lodgings; of the 2,665 sick in the stockade, many had been refused admission only because of congestion in the hospital. Out of 8,583 patients admitted during the month of May, 708 died; in June 1,201 cases terminated fatally out of 7,968 admissions. With a patient-doctor ratio of over two hundred to one, the chief surgeon recommended that ten additional doctors be assigned him.[1]

In late June White established "Sumter hospital" for the Confederate troops at Andersonville. Designed to accommodate one hundred patients, it could be staffed only by drawing upon the undermanned prison medical force. Apparently efficient operation of the prison hospitals was impeded by conflicting ideas of Surgeon White and Captain Wirz. Repeating his request for more medical officers, White asked also for "one or more good surgeons" to be placed in charge of different divisions in the prison hospital, adding that direct contact between Wirz and "the surgeon in charge of the prison hospital . . . would produce incalculable discord and confusion" unless the surgeon were "willing to co-operate and forego many things that would be desired for the proper arrangement of a hospital." Greatly discouraged by repeated failure in his efforts to get more tents, the chief surgeon observed that quartermasters "seem to have nothing or all act upon the principle that prisoners can do without them." No less serious was his inability to obtain sufficient medicines. On several occasions during the second quarter of 1864 the prison was completely without medicine of any kind.[2]

The ravages of smallpox among some of the prisoners transferred from Richmond in early spring induced the Andersonville authorities to establish a smallpox hospital a short distance northeast of the prison hospital. To help prevent spread of this disease the doctors vaccinated between two and three thousand prisoners who were without vaccine scars. Many of those inoculated were suffering from scurvy, and in most of these cases the pustule became ulcerated, the ulcer spread, and gangrene set in. Unless promptly arrested by proper drugs and diet which were usually not available, gangrene necessitated amputation of the arm. In many instances diarrhea and dysentery supervened* and the sufferer speedily perished. So numerous were amputations and deaths following the vaccinations that some prisoners mistakenly accused their captors of inoculating them with poison vaccine. In late April Chief Surgeon White reported smallpox on the decline, and although occasional cases continued to appear in the stockade for some time, the isolation of infected men and vaccina-

* Although diarrhea is only a symptom of numerous diseases, medical men at the time of the Civil War considered it a distinct "disease." They knew nothing of the bacterial or protozoal agents that cause dysentery, or of the spread of this infection by contaminated food and drink. To them dysentery was distinguished from diarrhea by ineffectual and painful straining and the presence of blood in the stool, but they used the two words almost interchangeably. See H. H. Cunningham, *Doctors in Gray: The Confederate Medical Service* (Baton Rouge, 1958), pp. 184, 186.

tion of others helped to bring the disease under control.[3]

When Colonel Chandler inspected Andersonville in early August, the prison hospital had 1,305 patients and fifteen doctors. Surgeon E. Sheppard ran the smallpox hospital, in which over half the patients admitted had died. Surgeon Erasmus D. Eiland and Assistant Surgeon W. H. Credille had charge of the first and second divisions of the prison hospital respectively. One assistant surgeon and one acting assistant surgeon were on duty in Sumter hospital, thirteen acting assistant surgeons took care of sick call for prisoners in the stockade, one was assigned to the First Georgia Reserves, one to the Engineer Corps, and one had the duty of purchasing supplies. The eight assistant surgeons and three surgeons, including Dr. White, held commissions as medical officers, but eighteen of the acting assistant surgeons were contract physicians, and the other six had been detailed from the militia by Governor Brown. Most of those employed by contract had engaged to practice at Andersonville only to avoid serving in the militia, while the detailed physicians had accepted their positions in order to escape service in the ranks; White expected to lose both groups as soon as the militia disbanded. But, according to Chandler, their loss would produce only slight injury, for they were "generally very inefficient," resided away from the post, visited it only once daily, and gave "but little attention to those under their care." He recommended that they be replaced by commissioned medical officers who should be required to reside at the post, but Samuel P. Moore, surgeon general of the Confederacy, replied that medical officers were "not to be had at present."

The morning report of August 2 showed 5,010 sick in the stockade in addition to the 1,305 in the hospital. The doctors attending sick call did not enter the prison. Each squad-sergeant reported at the gate each morning with the sick of his squad, many of whom were so ill that their friends had to carry them. Just outside the gate the doctors examined them and prescribed from the short list of medicines available; afterward the sick returned to their quarters. Late in the afternoon paroled prisoners working as clerks brought the prescribed medicines to the gate and turned them over to the

sergeants who delivered them to their respective squads. Each
day the surgeons admitted to the hospital as many of the
worst cases as could be accommodated, but lack of facilities
obliged them to return many critically ill prisoners to the
stockade. Further, so great was the number seeking treatment
every day that many of the weakest ones were unsuccessful in
their efforts to gain access to the doctors, although sick call
often lasted over six hours.[4]

In the hospital most of the bunks had two occupants each,
and many of the tents had no bunks, the post quartermaster
being unable to furnish materials for their construction. Dr.
White attempted to obtain straw for bedding, but the prevalence of vermin necessitated changing it fortnightly; this fact,
combined with constant increase in the number of sick, made it
impossible to procure an adequate supply. Consequently many
patients found themselves lying on the bare ground, and in
addition, some three hundred were without shelter of any
kind. Nearly all of the hospital stewards were paroled prisoners, but contrary to what might be expected, they were extremely negligent in providing for their sick comrades even
those meager comforts which adverse circumstances would
have permitted. The inferiority of hospital care and treatment, plus the necessity of admitting none except the most
critically ill, resulted in a ratio of deaths to admissions so high
that prisoners regarded admission to the hospital as a death
warrant.[5]

The chief surgeon complained of the system of filling requisitions for medical supplies. He drew his supplies from
Macon, but before requisitions from Andersonville were filled
they went to Atlanta for approval of the medical director.
Irregularity of mail deliveries frequently delayed their return
for as long as two weeks, and then the medical purveyor in
Macon was often unable to issue the quantities needed. White
suggested that the Macon purveyor be instructed to honor his
requisitions without approval from Atlanta. Concerning this
situation and suggestion Surgeon General Moore commented:
"Surgeon White was authorized some time since to send his
requisitions . . . direct to the medical purveyors. Not having
supplies is his own fault. He should have anticipated the wants
of the sick by timely requisitions."[6]

On August 6, Dr. White submitted to General Winder a report on the sanitary condition of the prison and pointed out certain evils which he considered "within the power of proper authorities to correct." He thought it possible to relieve the congestion, arrange the camp in order, "with streets of sufficient width to allow free circulation of air," construct barracks and hospital buildings, and improve the rations. White insisted upon the necessity for establishment and enforcement of stringent regulations regarding cleanliness and sanitation. Pointing to the filthy condition of the creek, he urged that Confederate troops be prohibited from polluting it above the stockade, that it be widened and deepened and its bottom and sides covered with planks, and that inviting "sinks" (latrines) be constructed where prisoners would not "have to wade through mud and faeces to use them." To halt the loathsome contamination of the entire stockade, White suggested that it might be necessary to instruct sentinels "to fire on anyone committing a nuisance in any other place than the sinks."[7]

Around the end of August, White assigned Dr. R. Randolph Stevenson to take charge of the prison hospital. Soon afterward White was promoted to chief surgeon and inspector of hospitals attached to military prisons in Georgia and Alabama, and Stevenson became "surgeon in charge" of hospitals at Andersonville. Upon assuming his new duties Stevenson gave the surgeon general a description of the stockade, the prison hospital, and the facilities at his disposal. He was shocked by the unsanitary conditions. "At all times of the day and night," he reported, "a most noisome stench arises from the decomposing excrementitious matter deposited in the prison and hospital grounds." Four barracks—shelter for 1,080 men—had been completed in the stockade, but Stevenson found "no building of any character whatever for the accommodation of the sick and wounded." Of the thirteen doctors assigned to stockade sick call, only four were on duty. The others, as well as half of the twenty-four on the hospital staff, were on sick leave or leave of indulgence. The contract physicians and doctors detailed from the militia were, in Stevenson's view, "as a matter of course . . . very inefficient." Proper care of the sick and wounded, he averred, required the services of at least thirty competent medical officers in the prison hospital and at least twenty-five in the stockade.[8]

Stevenson condemned the practice of using paroled prisoners as hospital stewards and suggested that replacing them with disabled Confederate soldiers would save property, provisions, and medicines. He considered the hospital cooking arrangements "very deficient" and the bread baked from unbolted meal "most unhealthy." In addition to bacon, beef, cornbread, and beans, hospital inmates frequently received rice, wheat bread, salt, and molasses, and occasionally green corn, vinegar, and sweet potatoes. By maintaining such diet and supplementing the medicines supplied by the medical purveyor with indigenous remedies, Stevenson thought it possible to reduce appreciably the mortality rate if proper hospital accommodations could be provided. "Great efforts have been made to make the stockade secure and prevent the escape of prisoners," he wrote, "and but little attention paid to the hygienic and sanitary condition of the sick." He requested that an efficient quartermaster and commissary be assigned to special hospital duty at Andersonville and empowered to "provide for the comfort of the sick and wounded Federal prisoners." Since one of the major obstacles to supplying their needs was the difficulty of getting transportation, Stevenson recommended that hospital stores be given transportation priority over everything except ammunition.[9]

Maintaining that is was impossible to keep tents properly policed in a hospital and asserting that shelter could be quickly and cheaply provided, Stevenson submitted a plan for forty hospital sheds, 100 by 22 feet and 8 feet high at the eaves, to be constructed on a plat measuring 450 by 900 feet. These structures were to have awnings made of old tents, which, he stated, were abundant. The hospital was to be divided into four divisions of ten sheds each, with fifty patients in each shed, making a total capacity of two thousand. Stevenson proposed a combination kitchen and convalescent dining room for each division, a special diet kitchen, a stockade around the entire hospital, and a storehouse for commissary supplies and medicines outside the stockade. Such a hospital would be the cheapest type for Andersonville, he declared, or for any other post "where lumber and material are so easily procured."[10]

The interest and labors of a scientific investigator resulted in an elaborate report of conditions in the prison hospital in September. Learning of the high mortality among the Andersonville prisoners, Surgeon Joseph Jones expressed to Surgeon General Moore "a desire to visit Camp Sumter, with the design of instituting a series of inquiries upon the nature and cause of the prevailing diseases." Born in Liberty County, Georgia, in 1833, Jones received his M.D. degree from the University of Pennsylvania, taught at Savannah Medical College and the University of Georgia, and was a professor of medical chemistry at the Medical College of Georgia in Augusta when the war began. He served six months as a private in the cavalry before being transferred to the medical service, in which he became a surgeon major. In early August, 1864, Surgeon General Moore directed him to "institute an extended investigation upon the causes, pathology, and treatment" of diseases affecting the prisoners confined at Andersonville. To Chief Surgeon White, Moore wrote:

> The field for pathological investigations afforded by the large collection of Federal prisoners in Georgia, is of great extent and importance, and it is believed that results of value to the profession may be obtained by a careful investigation of the effects of disease upon the large body of men subjected to a decided change of climate and the circumstances peculiar to prison life. The surgeon in charge of the hospital for Federal prisoners, together with his assistants, will afford every facility to Surgeon Joseph Jones, in the prosecution of the labors ordered by the surgeon general. Efficient assistance must be rendered Surgeon Jones by the medical officers, not only in his examinations into the causes and symptoms of the various diseases; but especially in the arduous labors of post mortem examinations.
>
> The medical officers will assist in the performance of such post mortems as Surgeon Jones may indicate, in order that this great field for pathological investigation may be explored for the benefit of the medical department of the Confederate army.[11]

When Jones arrived at Andersonville in early September, paroled Negro prisoners pitched a tent for him about one-eighth of a mile southwest of the depot and White and Stevenson provided him with the facilities needed for conducting his examinations in the prison hospital. But Wirz refused to grant him entrance to the stockade until ordered to do so by General Winder's assistant adjutant general. Jones spent about three weeks at the post before proceeding to Macon to investigate gangrene in the Army of Tennessee. The report of his Andersonville studies which he had just completed when the Confederacy collapsed never reached the surgeon general, for whose eye it was prepared. According to Jones's later statement, he filed it away intending to suppress its content, but "a distinguished member of the medical profession of the North" who had visited in his home after the war made its existence known to United States authorities, who seized it for use in the Wirz trial.[12]

Jones's description of the hospital is enough to explain the shocking mortality among its inmates. The lower portion of the stream flowing through the grounds, used by patients for excretion of wastes, he depicted as a semiliquid mass of filth which emitted an overwhelming stench. The noxious vapors from Stockade Creek, which issued from the stockade a short distance north of the hospital, added to the fetor. Referring to this miasmic swamp, Jones wrote: "As these waters, loaded with filth and human excrement, flow sluggishly through the swamp below, filled with trees and reeds coated with a filthy deposit, they emit an intolerable and most sickening stench. Standing as I did over these waters in the middle of a hot day in September, as they rolled sluggishly forth from the stockade, after having received the filth and excrement of twenty thousand men, the stench was disgusting and overpowering; and if it was surpassed in unpleasantness by anything, it was only in the disgusting appearance of the filthy, almost stagnant, waters moving slowly between the stumps and roots and fallen trunks of trees and thick branches of reeds, with innumerable long-tailed, large white maggots, swollen peas, and fermenting excrement, and fragments of bread and meat."

Enclosed by a flimsy board fence, the hospital contained about two thousand patients huddled together in ragged tents without bedding, many without bunks or even blankets. The tents extended almost to the cesspool on the east side, and near the spot where the cooking was done Jones observed a mound of "corn bread, bones, and filth of all kinds, thirty feet in diameter and several feet in height, swarming with myriads of flies." Flies crawled over the faces and in the open mouths of sleeping patients, depositing their eggs in open sores and wounds, and many patients were so nearly covered with mosquito bites that they presented the appearance of men suffering from measles. Paroled prisoners employed as hospital attendants stole money, rations, and clothing from the sick and dead and conducted a furtive trade with Confederate guards and with other paroled prisoners working outside the stockade. Dr. Jones reported hearing a sick prisoner whose arm had been wounded accuse one of the nurses, a fellow captive, of inoculating his wound with gangrene to kill him and acquire his clothing.

Many patients, the investigator reported, were "literally incrusted with dirt and filth and covered with vermin." The method of washing gangrenous wounds was simply to pour water over them, allowing the putrid matter to soak into the earth beside the board, blanket, or pile of rags on which the patient lay. Cloth for bandages was very scarce, and in dressing wounds attendants often used the same filthy rags several times without proper cleansing. Under these circumstances it was practically certain that all wounded patients would become infected with the prevailing hospital gangrene. In some cases gangrenous wounds were alive with maggots. Because maggots destroy dead cells without injuring healthy tissue, it was common medical practice at that time to use them for cleansing putrid wounds, and Jones seemed to think "that a gangrenous wound which had been thoroughly cleansed by maggots healed more rapidly than if it had been left by itself." This would have been true if the services of the maggots could have been utilized under sterile conditions. But the filth in which maggots thrived at Andersonville was conducive to innumerable infections.

The method of disposing of corpses had a most depressing effect on those who expected soon to be numbered among the dead. The deadhouse, located in the southwest corner of the hospital enclosure, was a wooden frame covered with bushes and pieces of old tents. Mother Earth was its floor, and most of the corpses were indescribably filthy. Dead bodies remained in the narrow streets running in front of the hospital tents until removed by paroled Negro prisoners detailed to dispose of the dead. Patients who died during the night lay in the streets until morning, and not infrequently during the day corpses remained there for hours.

Patients who were too sick to walk to the stream defecated into wooden boxes placed in the passages between rows of tents. Seldom were these boxes emptied before they were full. Being made of wood, they could not be properly cleansed. Many prisoners who appeared strong enough to walk to the stream without difficulty evacuated their bowels within their tents. "The whole soil," wrote Jones, "appeared to be saturated with urine and filth of all kinds. . . . The air of the tents was foul and disagreeable in the extreme, and in fact the entire grounds emitted a most nauseous and disgusting smell."

The hospital had only four large iron kettles for cooking the food of almost two thousand men, and patients relied chiefly on their own inadequate utensils. The practice of permitting them to cook inside their tents and in the narrow lanes produced more filth and further encouraged the breeding of vermin. The patients themselves seemed to be completely indifferent to the squalor, and the persons and clothing of most of them were extremely filthy and scaly with vermin. Frequently they were in a deplorable condition when admitted to the hospital. Jones reported seeing "men brought in from the stockade in a dying condition, begrimed from head to foot with their own excrements, and so black from smoke and filth that they resembled negroes rather than white men." The nurses seemed careless and inattentive rather than malevolent in their neglect of patients, and most of the abuses, Jones declared, resulted from "the absence of intelligent organization and division of labor," and "the almost total absence of system, government, and rigid but wholesome sanitary regulations."

According to Jones, 9,479 prisoners died between February 24, when the prison was established, and September 21. Thus in a period of slightly less than seven months, 23.3 per cent of those who had been confined at Andersonville had perished. During this period the monthly ratio of mortality increased from 3.77 per cent of the average number of sick and well prisoners in March to 9.09 per cent of the average number in August. The chief causes of "this extraordinary mortality" were "diarrhea, dysentery, scurvy, and hospital gangrene," and the main reason for the progressive increase of mortality was "the accumulation of the sources of the disease, as the increase of excrements and filth of all kinds and the concentration of noxious effluvia." Added to this were the effects of improper diet, congestion, and exposure.[13]

Medical records for the Confederate troops at Andersonville are far less complete than those for the prisoners, but they are sufficient to reveal a high death rate. During July and August 66.4 per cent of the command reported sick, and the mortality rate for this two-month period was 2.3 per cent of average strength. Such mortality, although less than 15 per cent of that among the prisoners during the same period, would completely obliterate an entire command in about seven and one-half years. Typhoid fever was almost three times as prevalent among guards as it was among prisoners, but the ratio of deaths to cases of this disease was slightly lower among the guards. Jones attributed the prevalence of sickness and disease among the Confederate troops to their extreme youth or advanced age and to the fact that they had only recently been exposed for the first time to the diseases that usually attack raw troops.

The death register indicated that the greatest killer among the prisoners was diarrhea, which was listed as the cause of 3,530 deaths in the six months from March 1 to September 1. Dysentery was named as the cause of death in 999 cases. These two ailments caused 58.7 per cent of the deaths during this six-month period, and practically every prisoner was affected to some extent by one of them. The main causes of bowel afflictions were, in Jones's opinion, "the long continued use of salt meat, and of coarse, unbolted corn bread, and improperly cooked food, and . . . the foul emanations from the all-abounding filth and excrements." In the same period 999 deaths were attributed to scurvy, and Jones expressed the conviction that a scorbutic condition made many prisoners easy prey to other diseases which caused death. In addition, he stated that many deaths listed under other causes were actually the result of diarrhea, dysentery, and scurvy. The prevalence of scurvy was a manifestation, Jones observed, of "the effects of salt meat and an unvarying diet of corn-meal, with but few vegetables and imperfect supplies of vinegar and sirup." Typhoid fever attacked 472 prisoners and caused 185 deaths, while of 2,958 cases of malarial fever, only 113 were fatal.

The malady to which Dr. Jones devoted most attention was hospital gangrene, about which he wrote after performing about twenty autopsies.

> In the foul atmosphere of the stockade and hospital, reeking with noxious exhalations, the smallest injury, as a splinter running into a hand or foot, the blistering of the arms or hands in the hot sun, or even the abrasions of the skin in scratching a mosquito bite, were often followed by the most extensive and alarming gangrenous ulceration . . . Numerous amputations have been performed in the hospital for gangrene supervening upon slight injuries, as the prick of a splinter, a scratch, or upon scorbutic ulcers.
>
> . . . From the sameness of the food and from the action of poisonous gases in the densely crowded and filthy stockade and hospital, the blood was altered in its constitution even before the manifestation of actual disease.
>
> . . . The exhalations from the hospital and stockade appeared to extend their effects to a considerable distance outside of these localities. Thus . . . Confederate soldiers . . . who did not enter the stockade . . . were in several instances attacked with hospital gangrene.
>
> . . . The origin of hospital gangrene . . . appeared clearly to depend in great measure upon the state of the general system. . . . The rapidity of the appearance and action of the gangrene depended upon the powers and state of the constitution, as well as upon the intensity of the poison in the atmosphere, or upon the direct application of poisonous matter to the wounded surface. . . . hospital gangrene, or a disease resembling it in all its essential respects, attacked the intestinal canal of patients laboring under ulceration of the bowels, although there were no local manifestations of gangrene upon the surface of the body. This mode of termination in cases of

dysentery was quite common in the foul atmosphere of the C. S. military prison hospital, in the depressed, depraved, condition of the system of these Federal prisoners.

. . . A scorbutic condition of the system appeared to favor the origin of foul ulcers, which frequently took on true hospital gangrene. Scurvy and hospital gangrene frequently existed in the same individual. In such cases vegetable diet with vegetable acids would remove the scorbutic condition without curing the hospital gangrene.

. . . Gangrenous spots, followed by rapid destruction of tissue, appeared in some cases when there had been no known wound . . . neither the contact of the poisonous matter of gangrene nor the direct action of the poisoned atmosphere upon the ulcerated surface is necessary to the development of the disease.

. . . In this foul atmosphere amputation did not arrest hospital gangrene; the disease almost invariably returned. Almost every amputation was followed finally by death, either from the effects of gangrene or from the prevailing diarrhea and dysentery.[14]

Having no knowledge of germs or the manner in which infections are actually transmitted and accepting the prevailing belief that noxious vapors in the air produced disease, Jones mistakenly concluded that the "foul atmosphere" was responsible for gangrene and that patients could develop the necrosis without contact.

Witnessing the misery in the prison hospital, Jones's secretary, Louis Manigault, wrote to his wife: "In my travels in China, and various sections of the Globe, I have witnessed many an awful sight, and beheld the dead and dying in various stages. I even now recall to mind most vividly some fearful scenes of death within the Prison at Shanghai, and also cases of Cholera in the North of China, but all is nothing to what I am now beholding."[15]

Feeling that "this gigantic mass of human misery calls loudly for relief," Jones recommended quadrupling of the hospital and prison areas, construction of shelter, improvements in diet, issue of cooking utensils, clothing, and bedding to the sick, use of disabled Confederates as nurses, appointment of chaplains, "thorough organization of the medical department with a large increase of medical officers," establishment of sanitary rules and regulations, and sufficient increase of the guard to insure enforcement of a rigid police system. Some idea of the attitude with which these suggestions were regarded by Samuel H. Stout, medical director of the hospitals of the Department and Army of Tennessee, under whose jurisdiction the hospitals at Andersonville were administered, may be obtained from his later comments on Jones. Stout wrote: "He was noted for a disposition to find fault, and never proposed a rational remedy for anything. He was . . . to be seen everywhere *flickering* about and furnishing aid no where to the over worked surgeons."[16]

About the time Jones began his studies at Andersonville, Surgeon General Moore instructed Dr. White to remove all the sick who could be transported without endangering their lives and to send the medical officers with them. For all practical purposes Andersonville ceased to be a receiving depot for prisoners and became primarily a prison hospital, with enough able-bodied prisoners retained to do most of the necessary labor. In early October Stevenson reported to General Winder that his plan for hospital sheds was being executed and that in another month he would have "ample accommodations" for two thousand patients if weather conditions permitted the work to proceed. But with such a high proportion of those left at Andersonville critically ill, the mortality rate rose markedly. To the 8,218 prisoners present on October 1, 444 were added during the month. Of these 8,662 men, 3,913 received treatment in the hospital and 1,560 died. Twenty-eight escaped and 2,866 were transferred to other prisons. If one-half the sum of prisoners on hand at the beginning of the month and prisoners on hand at the end of the month be taken as "mean strength,"* this would give a mor-

---

* Jones arrived at "mean strength" by adding together the number of prisoners on hand at the beginning, middle, and end of a month and dividing by three (see *Wirz Trial,* pp. 639-40). Stevenson reported 1,595 deaths in October (*O.R.,* Ser. 2, VII, 1075), but 1,560 is the figure given in Captain Wirz's consolidated return for the month (*Ibid.,* 1082-83) and in manuscripts in the National Archives.

tality rate for October of 25.1 per cent, as compared with 9.09 per cent for August.[17]

Although Stevenson appeared to be an energetic administrator, some of his colleagues became suspicious of his handling of the funds provided for outside purchase of articles which neither the commissary nor the medical purveyor could supply. Stevenson would not permit them to examine his statements. According to Assistant Surgeon G. G. Roy, the surgeon in charge had a sign over his door reading: "All persons not to enter unless on special business." But on December 20 General Winder ordered Stevenson to Columbia, South Carolina, and he was replaced by Dr. H. H. Clayton, who opened the books for inspection. Assistant Surgeon Amos Thronburgh testified at the Wirz trial that "large quantities of things" desperately needed by patients appeared on weekly statements when actually they had not been delivered.[18]

Informed of this situation, Medical Director Stout sent Surgeons E. A. Flewellen and E. S. Gaillard to investigate. Something in the neighborhood of $100,000 appeared to have been embezzled. Flewellen wrote Stout that he and Gaillard had "no doubt created quite a sensation" at Andersonville, "and one which will be felt by others now absent from that post." The Confederacy expired before the investigators could get around to making an official report, but Dr. Roy concluded from conversation with Flewellen and Gaillard that Stevenson was guilty of "gross fraud." This came as a great surprise to Roy, who wrote Stout that although he regarded Stevenson as "a *poor medical man* & no Surgeon," he had always considered him a gentleman and "honest in his efforts to promote the welfare of the sick." Roy had attributed Stevenson's failure to attend patients in the hospital to the fact that he was occupied with erection of hospital buildings. Supplies for sick prisoners had been so meager as to leave "the impression that no hospital fund had been received" during Stevenson's administration. "I very much regret," wrote Roy, "being connected with a hospital where such rascality has been practiced."[19]

The optimism which Stevenson expressed in October concerning completion of the hospital sheds was ill-founded. He continued to encounter difficulty in obtaining supplies, and although Clayton continued the project after Stevenson's departure, it was never completed. Under Clayton's administration, with fewer patients in the hospital, the supply of food and medicine was more adequate, and the mortality rate for the first quarter of 1865 declined to 3.14 per cent of mean strength.[20]

8

Trial and Judgment

BY THE END OF SEPTEMBER, 1864, most of the prisoners, armaments, and guards had been removed from Andersonville. General Winder transferred his headquarters to Camp Lawton and on October 9 assigned Colonel George C. Gibbs to command Camp Sumter in an order which specified that the prison and prisoners were to be in Wirz's charge and that no one should enter the prison without a pass from him. On November 21 Adjutant General Cooper made Winder commander of all Confederate prisons east of the Mississippi River.[1]

The movements of Union armies in Tennessee, Alabama, Florida, Georgia, and the Carolinas in late 1864 and early 1865 kept Confederate authorities guessing as to the safest place to keep prisoners of war. Expecting a raid on Andersonville from Sherman's army, they continued to send its inmates elsewhere until it became apparent that the Federals planned no movement in that direction. In early November Wirz complained of prisoners escaping every night because he had no "guard left to guard Stockade and Hospital both" and urged immediate removal of the remaining prisoners. At the end of the month he had only 1,359 captives on hand, but extensive raiding by General Judson Kilpatrick's cavalry soon caused concern for the security of some five thousand prisoners held at Thomasville; pursuant to orders of General P. G. T. Beauregard, commanding the Military Division of the West, Generals Winder and Cobb had about thirty-five hundred of them transferred to Andersonville, where they arrived on Christmas Eve.[2]

By this time Sherman had established his headquarters in Savannah, and Winder thought it might be wise to remove prisoners from South Carolina and North Carolina to Andersonville. Beauregard agreed that they should be moved but objected to having them all at one place. Cobb, closer to the Andersonville scene, was fearful of a Federal thrust on southwestern Georgia, which he styled "the granary at present of the Confederacy." Observing that the presence of prisoners at Andersonville increased the temptation to the enemy, he urged Beauregard to move them "if practicable." Disaffection was prevalent in the region and Cobb wrote President Davis that men of position and influence were participating in submission meetings. Georgians had learned to dread Sherman's "bummers," and a traveler expressed the opinion that it would be better to encounter the Yankees any other place "than here in South-West Georgia, for the horrors of the stockade have so enraged them that they will have no mercy on this country." Davis advised against sending more prisoners to Andersonville on the ground that it was unprotected.[3]

On every hand were signs that the Confederate sun was setting. Private I. R. S. Carroll, Company H, First Georgia Reserves, when arrested for selling whiskey to prisoners, readily confessed his guilt and blandly asserted that he had no idea he was doing anything wrong. Prisoners were paroled as drummers and fifers for the Second Georgia Regiment; without Wirz's knowledge these musicians trudged to a private home some five miles from Andersonville to serenade a lady who had given the regiment a flag. A prisoner from Dubuque, Iowa, succeeded in bribing a guard to mail an uncensored letter, and when a "Mrs. Spaulding" arrived at Andersonville in early January to visit this prisoner, Captain Wirz wrote a fellow-officer that he understood her to be the wife of a "prominent leader in the Union meeting to be held at Americus in a few days." A native Georgian who gave the name of Ann Williams arrived at Andersonville on the morning of January 15. Two days later Wirz reported as a fact "beyond doubt" that she had "sexual intercourse with at least seven prisoners." But she was not a prostitute, Wirz continued, for "on every occasion [she has] refused to take money, saying to them that she was a friend of theirs and had come for the purpose of seeing how she could help them."[4]

While Ann Williams sought to console the prisoners, Confederate officials sought means to prevent their escape. Asserting that Gibbs and Wirz had more troops than they needed, General Winder suggested that the excess reserves at Andersonville "might be profitably employed at Augusta." General Cobb inquired of Gibbs whether he could spare some troops and on February 13 requested him to send a part of his force to Augusta if he deemed it "consistent with the interest of the service."[5]

But Cobb was soon seeking troops for defense of southwestern Georgia against Union forces in eastern Alabama and northern Florida. Recruiting among Andersonville prisoners induced 138 captives to take the oath of allegiance to the Confederacy and enlist in its service.* Gibbs contributed a regiment and Cobb sent two hundred convalescents to Andersonville to be traded for reserves. When Gibbs objected to the swap, Cobb observed that he would change his mind when he saw how well the convalescents performed their duties, adding that the imminence of a general exchange of prisoners made an uprising less likely. On March 11 he informed Gibbs that the exchange was "about to be consumated" and ordered a stop to recruiting among the prisoners, since the exchange was to be on a man-for-man-basis. The next week Wirz began paroling prisoners for exchange on the Big Black River in Mississippi.[6]

General Sam Jones, who had been given command of the Military District of Florida, suggested sending the Andersonville prisoners to Jacksonville, Florida. General Gideon J. Pillow, who had become commissary general of prisoners after General Winder's death on February 6, asked the Union commander at Jacksonville, General E. P. Scammon, if he would accept them for exchange. Without hesitation Scammon agreed to receipt for them, but before any could be delivered he notified Jones that General Quincy A. Gillmore, Federal commander of the Department of the South, had ordered him to receive no prisoners without instructions from General

---

* A total of 338 Andersonville prisoners joined the Confederate army; 138 joined in March, 1865.

Grant. Some three thousand captives who were en route to Jacksonville had to return to Andersonville. Meanwhile Cobb was concentrating his meager forces at Columbus to repel the invader. In answer to his pleas for two reserve regiments, Colonel Gibbs replied that he had thirty-five hundred prisoners to guard and could send no troops to Columbus. Federal forces took Columbus on April 17 and about two weeks later Andersonville Prison came to an end. Colonel Gibbs wrote Cobb on May 4 that he had returned to Andersonville the previous day from Baldwin, Florida, where he had paroled all his prisoners for exchange. He continued: "I regret to inform you that in the absence of all guard a raid of soldiers, their wives, and the citizens was made upon the military stores last night and all the small amount here taken off. Government mules and everything in the way of provisions and unused clothing and bedding were taken from the quartermaster's and hospital departments."[7]

Months before the last Union prisoner left Andersonville, that pen of misery had become a subject of bitter controversy and it has remained so to this day, though happily the bitterness is now somewhat abated. In the late summer and early fall of 1864 reports of southern cruelty to prisoners of war had wide circulation in the North. The northern press called attention to liberally embellished accounts of conditions at Andersonville, and a people inflamed by the hatreds of war gave credit to stories of fiendish rebel guardians who subjected loyal men to inhuman tortures. Nor were these outrages attributed solely to the sadism of individual prison-keepers, for it seemed obvious to the victims and their countrymen that suffering on such a vast scale would have been impossible except by the design of Jefferson Davis and his colleagues. The intensity of northern feeling about Andersonville was well known in Georgia. The daughter of a Wilkes County judge wrote of hearing that Sherman had said he "did not intend to leave so much as a blade of grass in South-West Georgia," and that his men were so eager to avenge the ill-treatment of prisoners at Andersonville that he would be forced to order a raid on the place "to satisfy the clamors of his army, though he himself, the fiend Sherman, dreaded it on account of the horrors that would be committed." She expressed the firm conviction that "they will spare neither man, woman nor child in all South-West Georgia."[8]

Southerners a century ago, in defending their "peculiar institution" against the criticisms of the North and most of the Western world, felt obliged to defend slavery as a positive good, sanctioned by the Bible. In like manner supporters of the Lost Cause, in defending the Confederacy against northern accusations of barbarity and brutality, went too far in attempting to excuse the tragic episode at Andersonville.

It is true that the provocation was great. The North was in the grip of the understandable, though regrettable, hysteria which swept that section following Lincoln's assassination in the hour of victory over the hated rebellion. When General Winder died in February, 1865, Mary Boykin Chesnut, wife of a prominent Confederate leader, wrote: "Well, Winder is safe from the wrath to come. General [Mansfield] Lovell said that if the Yankees had ever caught Winder, it would have gone hard with him." But Henry Wirz, worn and haggard from lack of proper rest which the nagging pain in his arm would not permit, was still at Andersonville when Captain Henry E. Noyes arrived there in early May with orders for his arrest. Noyes took Wirz to Washington where a military commission tried, convicted, and sentenced him to hang for: (1) conspiring with Jefferson Davis, Howell Cobb, John H., Richard B., and W. S. Winder, Isaiah H. White, R. Randolph Stevenson, and others, to "impair and injure the health and to destroy the lives . . . of large numbers of federal prisoners . . . at Andersonville"; and (2) "murder, in violation of the laws and customs of war." Witnesses swore that they saw Wirz kill prisoners by striking, kicking, stamping, and shooting them in August, 1864, when he was away from Andersonville on sick leave, and the commissioners were sometimes grossly unfair to the defense in conducting the trial.[9]

The mere execution of Wirz, though an indefensible travesty of justice, probably would not have made many southerners feel the need to seek excuses for Andersonville. But in testimony presented at his trial, in articles published by northern newspapers and periodicals, in reminiscences of ex-prisoners, and in the speeches of politicians who sought to win votes by waving the "bloody shirt," the events that transpired at Andersonville were monstrously distorted, and the misery and suffering endured by thirty-two thousand Union soldiers, as well as the deaths of thirteen thousand others, were described as the result of a diabolical plot by Confederate leaders. The molders of public opinion so effectively impressed on the northern people the image of Andersonville as the acme of inhumanity that to this day the word itself remains to some a symbol of southern savagery.

During the war numerous southerners, particularly the people of southwestern Georgia, unhesitatingly expressed their commiseration for the unfortunate inmates of the stockade and denounced those responsible for permitting existence of such human wretchedness. Eliza Frances Andrews, an ardent rebel and a cultured southern belle who later became the first woman to be elected to membership in the International Academy of Literature and Science, wrote on January 27, 1865, after passing through Andersonville on the railroad: "It is dreadful. My heart aches for the poor wretches, Yankees though they are, and I am afraid God will suffer some terrible retribution to fall upon us for letting such things happen." Captain James M. Moore, who went to Andersonville in July, 1865, to mark the prisoners' graves and enclose the cemetery, reported encountering many Confederate veterans between Macon and Andersonville who readily conceded that the treatment of prisoners at Andersonville was a shameful stain on the record of the South.[10]

But such forthright criticisms shortly became unfashionable in the South because they seemed to weaken defense against northern accusations of deliberate brutality. In answering repeated charges of willfully exterminating prisoners of war, southerners attempted not only to vindicate the Confederacy for conditions at Andersonville but to shift the responsibility to the late enemy by attributing the suffering and death to the North's refusal to exchange prisoners. While it is doubtless true that exchanging prisoners would have prevented many of the deaths at Andersonville, it seems reasonable to assume that many of those exchanged would have been killed or maimed in battle and that unlimited exchange would have prolonged the war. Further, it is illogical to argue that since exchange would have saved lives, refusal to exchange *caused* deaths. The breakdown of exchange in no way relieved the South of its obligation under the recognized rules of war to care properly for prisoners. When a nation at war is no longer able to wage war, it is duty-bound to give up the struggle—as Robert E. Lee pointed out when urged to fight on with guerrilla tactics in April, 1865. If the Confederacy could no longer provide for its prisoners and was yet unwilling to surrender, it should have released them on parole— as both John Winder and Howell Cobb belatedly proposed.[11]

The two figures most closely associated with the prison— Wirz and Winder—have been the centers of heated and continuing controversy. Winder's accusers imputed to him the issuance of an order to the artillery to open fire on the stockade as soon as Stoneman's raiders were within seven miles of Andersonville. The statement that such an order was issued is pure fiction. Nor has any shred of credible evidence ever been produced to substantiate the charge that he desired to kill as many prisoners as possible or even that he was deliberately cruel to them. On the other hand, if he was greatly interested in ameliorating their condition, it was not evident to many of his southern contemporaries. In truth, Winder's true character was a puzzle to his contemporaries and remains an enigma to historians. It is possible that those who accused him during the war of inhumanity to prisoners misjudged him. A decade after the conflict James A. Seddon described him as "naturally somewhat abrupt and sharp" in his speech, suggested the possibility that "his military bearing may have added more of sternness and imperiousness," and stated his belief that Winder assumed these superficial traits "to disguise the real gentleness and kindness of his nature." Jefferson Davis in *The Rise and Fall of the Confederate Government* wrote that he was "too brave to be cruel to anything within his power, too well bred and well born to be influenced by low and sordid motives." The prison records reveal efforts of Winder to obtain materials which, if properly and efficiently used, might have improved the prisoners' conditions.[12]

Still it is evident that General Winder was ill-suited to the task assigned him. He was narrow, unimaginative, and shortsighted. In his relations with colleagues he was disputatious;

in handling subordinates he was inept. In prohibiting captives
from purchasing food from guards and citizens Winder was
acting in accordance with established usages governing the
administration of war prisons. Much was made in the Wirz
trial of his refusal to permit kind-hearted ladies to take vegetables into the stockade for the starving, scurvy-ridden prisoners. That this actually occurred is certified by descendants
of some of the women who thus sought to bring a small measure of relief to the prisoners. But one has only to recall
Winder's extravagant fear of a prison revolt and his firm
belief that the countryside was full of traitors to understand
his reason for denying the ladies admittance to the stockade.
He was doubtless afraid that these emissaries would give the
prisoners information calculated to facilitate an outbreak. Yet
by angrily asserting that the prisoners should not have the
delicacies and branding the angels of mercy as Yankee sympathizers, he convinced them that he was devoid of feelings
of humanity for the captives.[13]

To justify the legal lynching of Wirz, northerners called
him "the demon of Andersonville," "fiend incarnate," and
"human monster," and charged him with murdering helpless
prisoners in cold blood. In rejoinder, champions of the Confederacy represented him as a gentle, kind, compassionate
man—a "great martyr and grand hero." No one has offered
any proof that Wirz ever murdered a prisoner, but indu-
bitably he was harsh and rancorous in his demeanor and
unusually coarse in his speech. One official who inspected Andersonville later wrote that "he was exceedingly profane";
a member of the Fifty-fifth Georgia described him as "one
of the profanest men I ever saw" and alleged that cursing
"was his natural style of conversation"; one of General Winder's detectives averred that "he was an extremely profane
man and very strict in the discharge of his duties, oftentimes
severe toward prisoners"; and Wirz himself told of brandish-
ing his revolver and speaking to a prisoner "in a rough tone
of voice" and "in a menacing manner" and threatening to
kill him. Albert Bushnell Hart considered it anomalous that
"the South of Lee and Jackson and Sidney Johnston has
erected a monument to that man who performed no service
to the Confederacy except to be executed, who led in no

heroic action, represents no chivalry, and who did not so much as capture a color or an army wagon."[14]

Southerners have never been unanimous in venerating Wirz. In 1909 the Georgia Chapter of the United Daughters of the Confederacy unveiled a needle-like shaft in his honor in the center of the village of Andersonville, but one commentator declared that Confederate "veterans and many of the best citizens of the South" had been "shocked and grieved at the work of these women"; in 1958 the Georgia legislature voted sixty-eight to forty-four against a resolution to repair the monument. Opposition to the resolution was led by Representative Ulysses S. Lancaster, whose great-uncle, William Owens, served the Confederacy at Andersonville. Lancaster described Wirz as a malevolent sadist and affirmed that when Confederate veterans recalled "Wirtz and Andersonville it was with horror."[15]

Some descendants of Confederates who were with Wirz at Andersonville maintain that he was benevolent and humane, but others contend that he was a cruel fiend who delighted in seeing prisoners pursued by ferocious dogs or subjected to the tortures of balls and chains and the stocks. At best he was ill-natured and abusive, and the tormenting pain from his wound did nothing to improve his disposition. Although he was handicapped in his work by scarcity of able assistants, he was, like General Winder, a poor choice for the position he held. Yet a Richmond detective who knew him prior to his assignment to Andersonville professed the belief that those who spoke of his "inhumanity toward Federal prisoners" did so primarily "for the purpose of bolstering him as being a good officer."[16]

Any prison-keeper is apt to be disliked by those confined under his charge, and Wirz had qualities which kindled intense hatred in the minds of Andersonville captives. These same traits—plus the fact that Winder was dead—made him the cynosure of northern vindictiveness and set the stage for the farcical Wirz trial.

Many historians, seeking to be completely fair to both sides, have argued that the tragedy of Andersonville is simply an example of the fact that "war is hell" and that no one should be blamed for it. It is true that war was the great villain, but even though the sections were at war, the Confederate government should not have permitted the terrible conditions that existed at Andersonville. Many southerners have attributed those conditions to the scarcity of men, provisions, tools, and supplies, and there can be no doubt that the dearth of manpower and matériel which afflicted the Confederacy in its latter days was a factor in the suffering experienced by prisoners at Andersonville. But it is equally true that this suffering was due in part to the "quarrels and contentions" and the "gross mismanagement and want of system" which Major Turner pointed out in May, 1864. In attempting to fix the responsibility for Andersonville, one should weigh carefully the comment of prisoner David Kennedy: "What a degraded nation to hold prisoners and not provide for their wants." Those who revere the men who fought for southern independence should face up to the truth as did Eliza Frances Andrews, who wrote of Andersonville: "it is horrible, and a blot on the fair name of our Confederacy."[17]

Notes

CHAPTER 1

1. United States War Department, *The War of the Rebellion: A Compilation of the Official Records of the Union and Confederate Armies*, Ser. 3, V, 241; hereafter cited as *O. R.* (For additional source information, see the Bibliography.)

2. *O. R.*, Ser. 2, VI, 438–39, 455–56, 502.

3. William Best Hesseltine, *Civil War Prisons: A Study in War Psychology*, pp. 130–32.

4. *O. R.*, Ser. 2, VI, 558.

5. Ambrose Spencer, *A Narrative of Andersonville*, pp. 18–19. Spencer lived about nine miles from Andersonville at the time. See *The Trial of Henry Wirz*, 40th Cong., 2 sess., House Executive Document 23, p. 355; hereafter cited as *Wirz Trial*.

6. *Wirz Trial*, p. 43; John W. Northrop, "Diary of Prison Life at Andersonville During the Civil War," entry for May 24, 1864; hereafter cited as Northrop, "Diary."

7. J. Randolph Anderson to Lonnie G. Downs, January 18, 1947 (letter in possession of Mr. Downs, Montezuma, Georgia).

8. *Wirz Trial*, p. 372; Sumter County Deed Records, Book M, 95, Book N, 638, 639, Book O, 161.

9. *O. R.*, Ser. 2, VIII, 730–31.

10. Joseph Jackson Felder to Calvin W. Felder, December 15, 1863 (Joseph Jackson Felder Letters, Georgia State Archives).

11. Personal interview with Dr. Robert C. Pendergrass, January 20, 1959; Charlie Sheppard Pryor to Ivan Allen, Sr., October 7, 1957 (letter given to the writer by Mr. Allen).

12. *O. R.*, Ser. 2, VI, 965.

13. *Ibid.*, VII, 546, VIII, 595; R. Randolph Stevenson, *The Southern Side; Or Andersonville Prison*, p. 19; James Madison Page, *The True Story of Andersonville Prison: A Defense of Major Henry Wirz*, p. 61.

14. N. P. Chipman, *The Tragedy of Andersonville: Trial of Captain Henry Wirz, the Prison Keeper*, p. 470.

15. *O. R.*, Ser. 2, VI, 885–86.

16. Harrold Family Papers, Day Book, 1862–65, p. 426 (Emory University Library).

17. *O. R.*, Ser. 2, VI, 914.
18. *Ibid.*, 965–77.
19. *Ibid.*, 985.
20. *Ibid.*, 965–66.
21. *Ibid.*, 1043, 1054–55.
22. *Ibid.*, 996.
23. *Ibid.*, VIII, 731.
24. Sign at north end of Andersonville Prison Park.
25. John L. Ransom, *Andersonville Diary*, p. 42.

CHAPTER 2

1. *O. R.*, Ser. 2, VIII, 732.
2. Spencer, pp. 20–21; Warren Lee Goss, *The Soldier's Story of His Captivity at Andersonville, Belle Isle, and Other Rebel Prisons*, p. 76; Charles Fosdick, *Five Hundred Days in Rebel Prisons* (Chicago, 1887), pp. 24–26; Chipman, p. 52; M. V. B. Phillips, *Life and Death in Andersonville: Or, What I Saw and Experienced During Seven Months in Rebel Prisons* (Chicago, 1887), pp. 22–23; John McElroy, *Andersonville: A Story of Rebel Military Prisons*, p. 131.
3. *O. R.*, Ser. 2, VI, 1015.
4. *Ibid.*, VII, 40.
5. *Ibid.*, VI, 925; Horace Montgomery, *Howell Cobb's Confederate Career* (Tuscaloosa, Ala., 1959), p. 110.
6. *O. R.*, Ser. 2, VI, 925.
7. *Ibid.*, 993, 1042, VIII, 731; *Wirz Trial*, p. 99.
8. Ransom, p. 42; Spencer, p. 25; Page, p. 70; Eugene Forbes, *Diary of a Soldier and Prisoner of War in the Rebel Prisons*, p. 14.
9. Spencer, pp. 25–26.
10. *O. R.*, Ser. 2, VI, 1041–43.
11. Montgomery, pp. 113–14; Cobb to Cooper, April 4, 1864 (Cobb Letter Book, No. 55, Howell Cobb Papers, University of Georgia Library)—Unless otherwise specified, citations are to Cobb's letters in this book.
12. R. J. Hallett to Col. E. A. O'Neal, April 16, 1864 (Cobb Letter Book, No. 55).
13. Cobb to Cooper; Cobb to Mercer, April 19, 23, 1864.
14. Cobb to Mercer, April 26, 1864.
15. *Columbus Daily Enquirer*, April 14, 1864.
16. Cobb to Brown, April 24, May 12, May 23; to Cooper, April 28, 1864.
17. *Wirz Trial*, p. 100; see also *O. R.*, Ser. 2, VII, 136.
18. *O. R.*, Ser. 2, VII, 136.
19. Cobb to Cooper, May 2, 1864.
20. *Wirz Trial*, p. 706.
21. Wallace to his wife, August 21, 1865 (Wallace Papers, William Henry Smith Memorial Library, Indianapolis).
22. *Wirz Trial*, p. 706; National Archives, War Department Collection of Confederate Records, Record Group 109, General and Staff Officers' File, hereafter cited as Coll. Confed. Recs., R. G. 109; *O. R.*, Ser. 2, VII, 169.

23. *O. R.*, Ser. 2, VII, 169.

24. *Ibid.*, 89.

25. *Ibid.*, 207.

26. *Ibid.*, 120.

27. *Ibid.*, 99; for Bowie's report, see pp. 135–39.

28. Coll. Confed. Recs., R. G. 109, Ch. IX, V. 227, pp. 1, 13, 30.

29. *O. R.*, Ser. 2, VII, 92.

30. Bragg to Cobb (Cobb MS); Cobb to Persons.

31. Special Order No. 113 (Cobb MS).

32. Lamar Cobb to Persons to Aiken.

33. Cobb to Jackson, Lamar Cobb to Persons, May 23, 1864.

34. Lamar Cobb to Persons, May 24, 1864.

35. Cobb to Furlow, May 26, 1864.

36. For Turner's report see *O. R.*, Ser. 2, VII, 167–69.

37. *Columbus Daily Enquirer*, April 24, 1864; *O. R.*, Ser. 2, VII, 103; see also pp. 36, 52, 76, 110, 215.

38. Davis to Howell Cobb (telegram), June 3, 1864; S. Cooper to Cobb (telegram), June 4, 1864 (Cobb MS); *Augusta Daily Chronicle and Sentinel*, June 16, 1864; *O. R.*, Ser. 1, XXXIX, pt. 2, p. 634; Ser. 2, VII, 192.

39. Allen Johnson and Dumas Malone (eds.), *Dictionary of American Biography* (New York, 1936); hereafter cited as *DAB*.

40. Dunbar Rowland (ed.), *Jefferson Davis, Constitutionalist: His Letters, Papers, and Speeches* (Jackson, Miss., 1923), VII, 495.

41. "Resignation of Col. John H. Winder" (John H. Winder Papers, University of North Carolina Library). Unless otherwise specified, references to Winder's correspondence are found in this collection.

42. See J. G. Randall, *The Civil War and Reconstruction* (New York, 1937), p. 270.

43. Winder to Thomas, April 20, 1861; Thomas to Winder, April 30, 1861.

44. S. Cooper to Winder, June 21, 1861.

45. J. B. Jones, *A Rebel War Clerk's Diary at the Confederate States Capital* (Philadelphia, 1866), I, 59–60.

46. Jones, pp. 115, 116, 347, 348; *DAB*.

47. *DAB*; Jones, I, 114, 348; Edward Younger (ed.), *Inside the Confederate Government: The Diary of Robert Garlick Hill Kean, Head of the Bureau of War* (New York, 1957), pp. xxv–xxvi, hereafter cited as *Kean Diary*.

48. *O. R.*, Ser. 2, VII, 377.

CHAPTER 3

1. Ransom August Chadwick, "A Diary Kept in Andersonville Prison as a Member of the 85th New York Regiment, and a Few Miscellaneous Papers Relating to His Civil War Service," entries for June 1–17, 1864 (original in Minnesota Historical Society Library, microfilm in Emory University Library), hereafter cited as Chadwick, "Diary"; David Kennedy, "Diary of David Kennedy, Kept by Him While a Prisoner at Andersonville," entries for June 1–17, 1864 (copy in Minnesota Historical Society Library, microfilm in Emory University Library), hereafter cited as Kennedy, "Diary."

2. Kennedy, "Diary," May 17; Chadwick, "Diary," May 17; *O. R.*, Ser. 2, VII, 381, 386, 438.

3. Donald F. Danker (ed.), "Imprisoned at Andersonville: The Diary of Albert Harry Shatzel, May 5, 1864—September 12, 1864," p. 92, hereafter cited as "Shatzel Diary"; Forbes, p. 12; *Wirz Trial*, p. 176; Ransom, p. 48.

4. Chadwick, "Diary," May 22, 1864.

5. E. Merton Coulter (ed.), "From Spotsylvania Courthouse to Andersonville: A Diary of Darius Starr," p. 12, hereafter cited as "Starr Diary"; *O. R.*, Ser. 2, VII, 438; "Shatzel Diary," p. 107.

6. *O. R.*, Ser. 2, VII, 517.

7. "Shatzel Diary," p. 103; Kennedy, "Diary," June 3, 1864.

8. "Shatzel Diary," pp. 92, 101, 122.

9. *O. R.*, Ser. 2, VII, 138.

10. Kennedy, "Diary," May 7, 1864.

11. Forbes, p. 14; Chadwick, "Diary," June 5, 21, 26, July 6, 1864.

12. *Wirz Trial*, p. 111; *O. R.*, Ser. 2, VII, 1041; Ransom, p. 51; Forbes, pp. 12, 13, 18, 21, 22, 24, 26; Chadwick, "Diary," May 19, 1864; "Shatzel Diary," p. 99.

13. Forbes, p. 23.

14. *Ibid.*, pp. 18, 40; Ransom, pp. 69–70.

15. Forbes, pp. 11, 22, 23, 33, 35, 37.

16. C. M. Destler (ed.), "A Vermonter in Andersonville: Diary of Charles Ross, 1864," pp. 236, 240, hereafter cited as "Ross Diary"; "Starr Diary," pp. 11, 13, 15; Forbes, p. 38.

17. "Shatzel Diary," pp. 97–98, 101, 121–22.

18. Kennedy, "Diary," May 4, 5, 7, 8, 14, 23, 24, 29, 31, June 3, 5, 8, 14, 20, 27, July 1, 1864; "Starr Diary," p. 10.

19. Forbes, p. 18; *O. R.*, Ser. 2, VII, 438, 553.

20. Ransom, p. 44; Forbes, pp. 14, 15; Burdick, "Journal of Sergt. J. M. Burdick," July 25, 1864, hereafter cited as Burdick, "Journal."

21. Forbes, pp. 20–24, 26, 28–29, 31, 35–36, 39–41, 43; John A. Mendenhall, "Diary of J. A. Mendenhall," August 11, 1864, hereafter cited as Mendenhall, "Diary."

22. Chadwick, "Diary," July 1, 1864; Kennedy, "Diary," July 2, 1864.

23. Kennedy, "Diary," August 23–25, 1864; Ransom, p. 60.

24. Forbes, pp. 11, 24; "Shatzel Diary," p. 108; *Wirz Trial*, pp. 49, 63, 119; Chadwick, "Diary," June 27, July 2, 1864.

25. *O. R.*, Ser. 2, VIII, 599.

26. *Ibid.*, VII, 525.

27. "Shatzel Diary," pp. 92, 94.

28. Ransom, pp. 43, 50, 57; Forbes, p. 12; "Shatzel Diary," p. 98.

29. "Shatzel Diary," pp. 93, 96; Forbes, p. 17; Ransom, pp. 50, 57; Chadwick, "Diary," May 18, August 27, 1864; "Starr Diary," p. 10; Kennedy, "Diary," August 30, 1864.

30. Forbes, pp. 22, 41; *Wirz Trial*, pp. 36, 50, 128, 129, 140, 143, 171, 172, 178, 179–80; Spencer B. King, Jr., "Letter from an Eyewitness at Andersonville Prison, 1864," *Georgia Historical Quarterly*, XXXVIII (1954), 85, hereafter cited as "Letter from Andersonville."

31. Ransom, pp. 51–52; Mendenhall, "Diary," August 13, 1864; "Shatzel Diary," p. 98.

32. Ransom, p. 53.

33. Forbes, pp. 18–19, 22–23.

34. Ransom, pp. 43, 48, 51, 56; Forbes, pp. 16, 17, 18, 20, 23, 24, 27, 28, 40, 41, 42; "Shatzel Diary," pp. 95, 96–97; Chadwick, "Diary," June 9, 1864; "Ross Diary," pp. 235, 237.

35. *O. R.*, Ser. 2, VII, 617; Forbes, pp. 33, 34, 41; Ransom, pp. 55, 62; Louis Manigault Scrapbook, 1861–1865, p. 84, hereafter cited as Manigault Scrapbook.

36. Ransom, pp. 43, 44, 45, 47, 48, 52.

37. Kennedy, "Diary," May 9, 18, 20, 31, June 9, 1864.

38. *Ibid.*, June 24, 25, July 8, August 17, 1864; Ransom, pp. 45–46, 50.

39. *O. R.*, Ser. 2, VII, 618–21; Forbes, p. 31; "Shatzel Diary," p. 112; *New York Times*, August 30, 1864.

40. *O. R.*, Ser. 2, VII, 438, 517, 696, 708, VIII, 596.

41. Kennedy, "Diary," June 18, 1864; "Letter from Andersonville," p. 85.

42. Forbes, p. 36.

CHAPTER 4

1. Forbes, p. 13; "Starr Diary," pp. 10, 12; Chadwick, "Diary," June 24, 1864; "Shatzel Diary," p. 99; "Ross Diary," pp. 235, 237, 241.

2. Chadwick, "Diary," June 27, July 2, 12, 1864; "Starr Diary," p. 10; "Shatzel Diary," pp. 92, 93, 98; Forbes, pp. 11, 17, 27.

3. Ransom, p. 44; Chadwick, "Diary," July 5, 1864; "Shatzel Diary," p. 108; "Ross Diary," p. 240; "Starr Diary," p. 13; Kennedy, "Diary," May 29, 1864.

4. Ransom, pp. 41, 42, 47, 54.

5. Burdick, "Journal," July 12, 28, August 4, 1864; Kennedy, "Diary," May 11, 1864; "Shatzel Diary," pp. 115–16, 120.

6. Ransom, p. 43; McElroy, pp. 342–44; Forbes, pp. 18, 22.

7. Chadwick, "Diary," May 17—September 5, 1864, *passim*; Kennedy, "Diary," May 4—September 6, 1864, *passim*; Burdick, "Journal," July 31, August 20, 31, September 2, 1864; Forbes, pp. 11–46, *passim*; Ransom, pp. 42–43; McElroy, pp. 154–55; "Ross Diary," p. 239.

8. Chadwick, "Diary," May 27, June 22, July 10, September 2, 1864; Kennedy, "Diary," May 17, 26, July 20, 28, 29, September 5, 1864; "Shatzel Diary," p. 93.

9. Ransom, pp. 43, 46, 47, 50, 52, 54, 58, 60; McElroy, pp. 324–29; Forbes, pp. 12–13, 16, 20, 21; Chadwick, "Diary," May 25, 1864.

10. Nat. Arch., War Dept., Commissary General of Prisoners, R. G. 249, "Andersonville, Ga. Rolls of Deceased Federal Prisoners, 1864–65," Box No. 20; *O. R.*, Ser. 2, VII, 438, 517, 708; Forbes, p. 16; "Shatzel Diary," p. 96; *Columbus Daily Enquirer*, May 12, 1864.

11. Ransom, p. 47; Forbes, pp. 12–13; McElroy, pp. 175–78; Robert H. Kellogg, *Life and Death in Rebel Prisons*, pp. 118–21.

12. "Shatzel Diary," pp. 112, 113.

13. Forbes, p. 16; Ransom, p. 69.

14. Ransom, pp. 50, 52.

15. Forbes, pp. 20, 22, 32.

16. Lawrence E. Hinkle, Jr. and Harold G. Wolff, "Communist Interrogation and Indoctrination of 'Enemies of the State,'" *A.M.A. Archives of Neurology and Psychiatry,* LXXVI (1956), 130, 170–71; Bruno Bettelheim, "Individual and Mass Behavior in Extreme Situations," *Journal of Abnormal and Social Psychology,* XXXVIII (1943), 438–39, 447.

17. "Shatzel Diary," pp. 101, 103.

18. Burdick, "Journal," July 16, 1864; Forbes, p. 31.

19. Ransom, pp. 56–57; see also K. C. Bullard, *Over the Dead-Line, Or Who Killed "Poll Parrot,"* pp. 16–17, 31–32.

20. Chadwick, "Diary," May 25, 1864; Kennedy, "Diary," May 27, 1864; Ransom, pp. 65–66; McElroy, pp. 193–94; Kellogg, pp. 105–6.

21. Forbes, p. 30.

22. McElroy, p. 196; Chadwick, "Diary," July 14, 1864.

23. Forbes, p. 30; "Shatzel Diary," p. 112; see also Kennedy, "Diary," July 14, 1864.

24. "Shatzel Diary," pp. 91–92; Ransom, p. 47; Kennedy, "Diary," May 25, 1864; Forbes, p. 34.

25. May 7, 9, 1864 (MS in possession of Charles T. Winship, Atlanta, Georgia).

26. *O. R.,* Ser. 2, VII, 403.

27. Forbes, pp. 12, 18, 21, 22, 25, 26, 27, 29, 30–31, 33, 34, 35, 36, 40, 41, 43, 45; "Shatzel Diary," pp. 94, 100, 104–5, 115; Kennedy, "Diary," June 22, July 4, 18, 27, August 2, 1864; Chadwick, "Diary," May 2, July 13, 1864; "Starr Diary," p. 12; Daniel and James Buckley, "Diary-Journal of Daniel and James Buckley," August 6, 1864 (Illinois State Historical Library), hereafter cited as Buckley, "Diary-Journal"; *Wirz Trial,* p. 497; Ransom, p. 86.

28. Ransom, pp. 44, 78; "Reminiscence of Mrs. Florence Hollis," July 20, 1929 (copy in possession of Dr. Robert C. Pendergrass, Americus, Georgia).

29. Ransom, pp. 46, 50, 68; "Ross Diary," pp. 236, 240; "Shatzel Diary," pp. 122, 123; McElroy, p. 214; Forbes, p. 20; Northrop, "Diary," May 25, 1864.

30. Coll. Confed. Recs., R. G. 109, Ch. IX, V. 227, pp. 1, 13, 30, 33, 35; Forbes, pp. 12, 16, 18, 20, 39–40; "Starr Diary," p. 10; Ransom, pp. 54, 70, 74, 92; King, pp. 395–98; Manigault Scrapbook, pp. 219–24; W. R. Worth to Mrs. William Worth, July 8, 1864 (Louis A. Bringier Papers, Louisiana State University).

31. Ransom, p. 69; James T. Harnit to Albert R. Kelly, November 15, 1864 (Ohio Historical Society); S. J. Gibson to Mrs. Rachel A. Gibson, June 12, 1864 (Manuscripts Division, Library of Congress).

32. Ransom, pp. 46, 48, 50, 61; McElroy, pp. 213–14; Chadwick, "Diary," June 2, 1864; Forbes, pp. 15, 17, 23; *New York Times,* September 5, 1864.

33. Kennedy, "Diary," May 15, June 5, 12, 26, July 31, August 14, 28, 1864; Ransom, p. 47; *Wirz Trial,* pp. 287, 293, 426, 430; Forbes, p. 32; Chadwick, "Diary," July 3, 1864.

34. Ransom, p. 47; Forbes, p. 32; Eliza F. Andrews, *The War-Time Journal of a Georgia Girl, 1864–1865* (New York, 1908), pp. 77–78; *Wirz Trial,*

p. 290; *Annales de la Propagation de la Foi,* XXXVII (1865), hereafter cited as *Annales.*

35. *Wirz Trial,* pp. 290, 293, 426, 430; *Annales,* p. 398.

36. *Wirz Trial,* pp. 609-10; Forbes, p. 35; Chadwick, "Diary," August 1, 1864; J. William Jones, *Christ in the Camp, or Religion in the Confederate Army* (Atlanta, 1904), p. 624.

37. Ransom, p. 47; Forbes, pp. 27, 28, 31, 32, 38; Mendenhall, "Diary," August 20, 1864; T. J. Shepherd, "Religious Life and Work in Andersonville," in McElroy, pp. 629-36; John W. Urban, *In Defense of the Union, or, Through Shot and Shell and Prison Pen,* p. 210.

CHAPTER 5

1. Ransom, p. 45.
2. Northrop, "Diary," May 5, 24, June 17, 28, 1864.
3. Northrop, "Diary," May 25, 1864.
4. Ransom, pp. 55-56; Northrop, "Diary," May 26, 1864.
5. Northrop, "Diary," May 27, 1864.
6. *Ibid.,* June 15, 1864.
7. Ransom, pp. 61, 67, 68, 71, 72.
8. Northrop, "Diary," June 28, 1864; Chadwick, "Diary," June 29, 1864.
9. Forbes, pp. 25-26; "Shatzel Diary," p. 106; Chadwick, "Diary," June 29, 1864; Ransom, pp. 72, 75-76; Northrop, "Diary," June 29, 1864.
10. Forbes, p. 25; *Wirz Trial,* p. 697.
11. Forbes, p. 25.
12. Northrop, "Diary," June 29, 1864; "Shatzel Diary," p. 106.
13. Northrop, "Diary," June 29, 1864; Forbes, pp. 25, 26.
14. Forbes, p. 26; Ransom, p. 76; Northrop, "Diary," June 30, 1864.
15. Forbes, pp. 25-26; Northrop, "Diary," June 29, 1864.
16. *O. R.,* Ser. 2, VII, 426.
17. Forbes, pp. 26-28; Northrop, "Diary," June 30, 1864; Ransom, p. 77.
18. *Wirz Trial,* p. 428; Northrop, "Diary," July 11, 1864; McElroy, p. 243.
19. *Wirz Trial,* p. 428. For slightly different versions of Wirz's remarks, see Northrop, "Diary," July 11, 1864, and McElroy, p. 244.
20. Forbes, p. 29; *Wirz Trial,* p. 428; Ransom, p. 82.
21. Ransom, pp. 82-83.
22. "Shatzel Diary," p. 111; see also Buckley, "Diary-Journal," July 11, 1864; Forbes, p. 29; Chadwick, "Diary," July 11, 1864; Kennedy, "Diary," July 11, 1864; "Starr Diary," pp. 13-14.
23. Forbes, p. 29.

CHAPTER 6

1. *O. R.,* Ser. 2, VII, 378, 381; Cobb to Winder, June 21, to Davis, June 24, 1864.
2. *O. R.,* Ser. 2, VII, 378, 386, 392.
3. Cobb to Davis, June 24, 1864.
4. *O. R.,* Ser. 2, VII, 393, 396.
5. *Ibid.,* pp. 410-11.
6. Winder to Cobb, July 9, 1864 (Cobb MS).

7. *O. R.,* Ser. 2, VII, 445; Cobb to Winder, July 8, 1864.

8. *O. R.,* Ser. 2, VII, 480.

9. *Ibid.,* 400-401, 417, 420, 451; Cobb to Winder, June 27, 1864.

10. *O. R.,* Ser. 2, VII, 499-500.

11. *Ibid.,* 436-37, 601-2.

12. Cobb to Winder, July 8, 1864; *O. R.,* Ser. 1, XXXVIII, pt. 5, 877; Ser. 2, VII, 458.

13. *O. R.,* Ser. 1, XXXVIII, pt. 2, 904-11.

14. General Henry R. Jackson to Cobb (telegram), Jones to Cobb (telegram), July 18, 1864 (Cobb MS); Cobb to Winder, July 18, 1864.

15. "Shatzel Diary," p. 114; see also Forbes, pp. 32-34; Chadwick, "Diary," July 22, 1864; Kennedy, "Diary," July 20, 21, 23, 25, 1864; "Ross Diary," pp. 235, 236; Burdick, "Journal," July 20, 22, 30, 1864.

16. Hood to Cobb (two telegrams), July 18, 1864, W. W. Mackall to Cobb (telegram), July 19, 1864, F. A. Shoup to Cobb (telegram), July 26, 1864 (Cobb MS); Cobb to Hood, July 26, 1864.

17. Brown to Cobb (telegram), July 26, 1864 (Cobb MS); Cobb to Winder, July 26, 1864.

18. *O. R.,* Ser. 2, VII, 490-91, 500.

19. *Ibid.,* Ser. 1, XXXVIII, pt. 1, 75-76; F. A. Shoup to Cobb (telegram), July 28, 1864 (Cobb MS).

20. *O. R.,* Ser. 2, VII, 503–4; "Shatzel Diary," p. 116; Forbes, pp. 34–36; Buckley, "Diary-Journal," July 28, 1864.

21. Winder to Cobb (two telegrams), July 30, 31, 1864, Winder to Colonel George C. Gibbs (telegram), August 1, 1864 (Cobb MS); *O. R.,* Ser. 1, XXXVIII, pt. 2, 748, 804, 813, 843, 854, 914-19, pt. 3, 688-89, 953-57.

22. F. A. Shoup to Cobb (telegram), August 10, 1864 (Cobb MS); Forbes, pp. 38-40, 42-43; "Shatzel Diary," p. 119; *O. R.,* Ser. 2, VIII, 111; Coll. Confed. Recs., R. G. 109, Ch. IX, V. 227, p. 27.

23. Cobb to Winder, August 9, 1864, Cobb to Seddon, August 20, 1864; *O. R.,* Ser. 1, VII, 546, 585-86.

24. Cobb to Winder, August 11, 17, 1864, R. J. Hallett to Winder, August 23, 1864, Cobb Letter Book, No. 55; F. A. Shoup to Cobb (two telegrams), August 15, 28, 1864, Hood to Cobb (telegram), August 28, 1864; *O. R.,* Ser. 1, XXXVIII, pt. 5, 998, 1025.

25. Cobb to Winder, October 29, 1864.

26. Cobb to Cooper, December 22, 1864; *O. R.,* Ser. 2, VII, 762.

27. *O. R.,* Ser. 2, VII, 546-52.

28. *Ibid.,* 550, 713, 755.

29. *Ibid.,* 756-62, 1091, 1114, 1156.

30. *Kean Diary,* p. 227n; Hesseltine, p. 149n.

31. Hesseltine, p. 153; *O. R.,* Ser. 2, VIII, 526-29.

32. *O. R.,* Ser. 2, VII, 756.

33. *Kean Diary,* pp. 227-29; R. G. H. Kean to Reverend J. William Jones, March 22, 1867, in Stevenson, pp. 467-72; *Wirz Trial,* pp. 309-10; Ben Ames Williams (ed.), *A Diary from Dixie* by Mary Boykin Chesnut (Cambridge, Massachusetts, 1949), pp. 475, 476.

34. Forbes, p. 37; Chadwick, "Diary," August 9, 1864; "Shatzel Diary," p. 118; "Ross Diary," p. 237; Burdick, "Journal," August 9, 1864; *O. R.,* Ser. 2, VII, 583-84, 586, 588-89.

35. *O. R.,* Ser. 2, VII, 546, 624-25, 762; Forbes, p. 37; "Shatzel Diary," p. 118; Burdick, "Journal," August 11, 1864.

36. Forbes, pp. 42, 44; Cobb to John H. Winder, September 6, 1864; *O. R.,* Ser. 2, VII, 782, 783, 821; Chadwick, "Diary," September 7, 1864; Kennedy, "Diary," September 7, 1864; "Shatzel Diary," p. 124; "Ross Diary," p. 239; Mendenhall, "Diary," September 7, 1864; Burdick, "Journal," September 7, 1864.

CHAPTER 7

1. *O. R.,* Ser. 2, VII, 386-87; VIII, 603-8.

2. *Ibid.,* VII, 417-18, 426-27.

3. Joseph Jones, *Medical and Surgical Memoirs,* pp. 396-97, 408, hereafter cited as Jones, *Memoirs; Wirz Trial,* pp. 45-680 *passim; O. R.,* Ser. 2, VII, 89; Ransom, p. 54; Chadwick, "Diary," May 14, 27, 1864; Joseph K. Barnes (ed.), *The Medical and Surgical History of the War of the Rebellion* (Washington, 1870-1883), I, pt. 3, 628, hereafter cited as *Med. and Surg. Hist.*

4. *O. R.,* Ser. 2, VII, 524-26, 547-48, 760; *Wirz Trial,* p. 381.

5. *O. R.,* Ser. 2, VII, 524-25, 547, 558; Ransom, pp. 48, 51; Forbes, p. 23; Kennedy, "Diary," June 10, 23, 1864.

6. *O. R.,* Ser. 2, VII, 387, 427, 525-26.

7. *Ibid.,* 557-60.

8. Isaiah H. White to Samuel H. Stout, October 31, 1864, Samuel H. Stout Microfilm, Fifth Series (Emory University Library), hereafter cited as Stout Microfilm; *O. R.,* Ser. 2, VII, 711, 830–31, 1075, 1169.

9. *O. R.,* Ser. 2, VII, 831-32; Commissary General of Prisoners, R. G. 249, Provision Returns for Camp Sumter Military Prison Hospital, August, 1864.

10. *O. R.,* Ser. 2, VII, 711.

11. Stevenson, p. 31; *Wirz Trial,* pp. 618–20; *DAB,* X, 193.

12. Manigault Scrapbook, p. 91; *Wirz Trial,* pp. 620, 641-42; Stevenson, pp. 32-34; Jones, *Memoirs,* p. 398; for Jones's report, see *O. R.,* Ser. 2, VIII, 588-632.

13. *Ibid.,* VII, 1012, VIII, 614-15; Manigault Scrapbook, p. 137.

14. *O. R.,* Ser. 2, VIII, 618-23.

15. "Letter from Andersonville," p. 84.

16. *O. R.,* Ser. 2, VIII, 623-25; Memoranda of Stout (Samuel H. Stout Papers, Emory University Library), Box No. 4.

17. *O. R.,* Ser. 2, VII, 817, 923, 1075-76, 1082-83; "Andersonville, Ga. Rolls of Deceased Federal Prisoners, 1864-65."

18. G. G. Roy to Samuel H. Stout, March 7, 1865, Stout Microfilm; Stevenson, p. 90; *Wirz Trial,* p. 335.

19. *Wirz Trial,* pp. 83-85, 334-35, 341-42, 382, 474, 477-78, 669, 671; Flewellen to Stout, March 3, 1865, Roy to Stout, March 7, 1865, Stout Microfilm.

20. *O. R.,* Ser. 2, VII, 1076; *Wirz Trial,* pp. 30-31, 40, 82-83; "Andersonville, Ga. Rolls of Deceased Federal Prisoners, 1864-65."

CHAPTER 8

1. "Andersonville, Ga. Rolls of Deceased Federal Prisoners, 1864-65", *O. R.,* Ser. 2, VII, 837, 869-70, 960, 1051, 1193.

2. *O. R.,* Ser. 2, VII, 1144-45, 1238-39, 1258; "Andersonville, Ga. Rolls of Deceased Federal Prisoners, 1864-65"; Beauregard to Cobb (telegram), December 17, 1864, H. W. Fielder to Cobb (telegram), December 22, 1864 (Cobb MS); Lamar Cobb to George C. Gibbs, December 19, 1864.

3. *O. R.,* Ser. 2, VII, 1302-4; Pope Barrow to Gibbs, R. J. Hallett to Gibbs, Cobb to Beauregard, December 26, 1864, Cobb to Colonel John M. Otey, December 28, 1864; Cobb to Davis, January 6, 1865 (Howell Cobb Letters, Duke University); Andrews, p. 64.

4. Coll. Confed. Recs., R. G. 109, Ch. IX, V. 227, pp. 21, 23–26, 33–34.

5. *O. R.,* Ser. 2, VIII, 126-27; R. J. Hallett to Gibbs, January 31, 1865; R. J. Hallett to Gibbs, February 13, 1865 (Cobb Letter Book, No. 59).

6. Cobb to General Lucius J. Gartrell, March 8, 9, 10, 13, 1865, Cobb to Gibbs, March 10, 1865, R. J. Hallett to Gibbs, March 11, 14, 1865, Hallett to Gartrell, March 14, 15, 1865 (Cobb Letter Book, No. 59); "Andersonville, Ga. Rolls of Deceased Federal Prisoners, 1864-65"; Coll. Confed. Recs., R. G. 109, Ch. IX, V. 227, pp. 36–37; *O. R.,* Ser. 2, VIII, 515.

7. *O. R.,* Ser. 2, VIII, 426, 427, 437, 445, 470, 532; R. J. Hallett to Lucius J. Gartrell, Hallett to Gibbs, April 13, 1865 (Cobb Letter Book, No. 59); Gibbs to Hallett, April 15, 1865 (Cobb MS).

8. Andrews, p. 65.

9. *Diary from Dixie,* pp. 475-76; Commissary General of Prisoners, R. G. 249, "Andersonville, Ga.; Military Prison"; Samuel Boyer Davis, *Escape of a Confederate Officer from Prison,* pp. 22, 33; *O. R.,* Ser. 2, VIII, 783–94; *Wirz Trial,* pp. 3-8, 18-20, 805-15.

10. *Augusta Daily Chronicle and Sentinel,* September 4, 9, 1864; Andrews, p. 78; *O. R.,* Ser. 3, V, 319–22.

11. *O. R.,* Ser. 2, VII, 1304; Cobb to James A. Seddon, September 9, 1864.

12. Samuel Davis, pp. 36-42; *Augusta Daily Chronicle and Sentinel,* September 9, 1864; *Wirz Trial,* p. 245; Seddon to W. S. Winder, December 29, 1875, in Stevenson, pp. 473-75; Jefferson Davis, *The Rise and Fall of the Confederate Government,* II, 597.

13. Daniel G. Gilman (ed.), *Miscellaneous Writings of Francis Lieber* (Philadelphia, 1881), II, 257-62; personal interviews with Mrs. J. Willis Shiver, January 20, 1959, Mrs. Ida Lee Janes and Mr. U. S. Lancaster, January 27, 1959, Mr. Bob English, January 30, 1959.

14. Robert M. Howard, *Reminiscences* (Columbus, Georgia, 1912), p. 247; unknown writer to Samuel H. Stout, May 18, 1874 (Stout Papers, Box No. 4); *Wirz Trial,* pp. 507-8, 711; *O. R.,* Ser. 2, VIII, 754; Albert Bushnell Hart, *The Southern South* (New York, 1910), p. 89.

15. Howard, pp. 244-45; *Atlanta Constitution,* February 5, 6, 20, 21, 1959.

16. Personal interviews with Mr. Harold Collins, May 24, 1957, Mrs. Ivaline Dunaway and Mr. Severs James Clark, September 27, 1957, Mr. Robert D. Branan, January 11, 1959, Mrs. Ida Lee Janes and Mr. U. S. Lancaster, January 27, 1959; *O. R.,* Ser. 2, VIII, 754.

17. Kennedy, "Diary," June 11, 1864; Andrews, p. 64.

Bibliographical Essay

FOR THE STUDY of Andersonville Prison the most valuable colections of manuscripts are the Howell Cobb Papers, Special Collections Division, University of Georgia Library, Athens, and the War Department collections in the National Archives, Washington. The Cobb Letter Books contain copies of letters sent from Cobb's office, while incoming communications are found in the Cobb Manuscripts, owned by Howell Cobb's grandson, Mr. Will Erwin, Athens. These sources shed considerable light on problems connected with guarding the prison. In the War Department Collection of Confederate Records, Record Group 109, are registers of letters received by the Confederate secretary of war and the adjutant and inspector general, an index to the register of letters received by the secretary of war, a Staff File on Henry Wirz, and one of Wirz's Andersonville letter books. The Andersonville death register, original burial list, and provision returns for the prison hospital, smallpox hospital, acting assistant surgeons, and hospital attendants are in Record Group 249, War Department, Commissary General of Prisoners. In the same group are the register of prisoners confined at Andersonville, the roll of Andersonville prisoners who joined the Confederate army, Andersonville hospital records, and a manuscript history of the prison, with a tabulated statement of the number of prisoners received, transferred, exchanged, escaped, and deceased.

The John H. Winder Papers, Southern Historical Collection, University of North Carolina, Chapel Hill, consist of forty-one pieces covering the years 1808-89 but deal mostly with Winder's pre-Civil-War career. Also in the Southern Historical Collection are the Samuel Hollingsworth Stout Papers, containing a small amount of information on hospital administration at Andersonville. Among the contributors to the collection of "Reminiscences of Confederate Soldiers," Georgia State Archives, Atlanta, were a few men who served at Andersonville, but their accounts are extremely brief and so marred by inaccuracies as to be practically worthless to the historian. The Harrold Family Papers, Special Collections, Emory University Library, Atlanta, include daybooks showing the sale of provisions to the Andersonville Prison authorities. One man's view of Wirz, with glimpses behind the scenes of the Wirz trial, are shown in letters written by General Lew Wallace, found in the Lew Wallace Papers, William Henry Smith Memorial Library of the Indiana Historical Society, Indianapolis.

Unpublished Diaries and Reminiscences

The diaries of Ransom August Chadwick and David Kennedy have proven especially helpful in studying the conditions of life in the Andersonville stockade. Chadwick's diary and a typed copy of Kennedy's are in possession of the Minnesota Historical Society, Minneapolis. Other unpublished diaries that have been useful are: "Diary of J[ohn] A. Mendenhall," William Henry Smith Memorial Library of the Indiana Historical Society; John W. Northrop, "Diary of Prison Life at Andersonville During the Civil War," Western Reserve Historical Society, Cleveland; Daniel and James Buckley, "Diary-Journal of Daniel and James Buckley," Illinois State Historical Library, Springfield; and J. M. Burdick, "Journal of Sergt. J. M. Burdick," in possession of Mr. Richard J. Harris, Swainsboro, Georgia.

The frailties of memory and the human tendency to magnify certain experiences and minimize others make the use of reminiscences a precarious endeavor. Although not dependable for factual details, accounts by ex-prisoners provide interesting examples of lingering mental impressions left by their prison experiences. The Connecticut State Library, Hartford, has manuscript accounts of prison life at Andersonville by three Connecticut soldiers: Norman L. Hope, "The Story of Andersonville"; Weston Ferris, "Prison Life of Weston Ferris, Troop B, 1st Conn. Cavalry"; and Albert A. Hyde, "Life of a Connecticut Soldier in a Confederate Prison During the Stormy Days of the War." The manuscripts of the Illinois State Historical Library, Springfield, include reminiscences of three Andersonville survivors: James Jennings, "A Story of the Trials and Experiences of James Jennings, Late of Co. K, 20th Infantry, at Andersonville Prison During the Civil War"; Stephen E. Payne, "Recollections of Experiences in Confederate Prisons"; and Winfield Scott Neely, "Reminiscences of Eighteen Months' Sojourn in Confederate Prisons." A copy of George W. Pease, "History of My Imprisonment in, and Escape from Andersonville Prison During the Summer of 1864" is in possession of the State Historical Society of Wisconsin, Madison.

Other Unpublished Sources

The Louis Manigault Scrapbook, covering the Civil War years, is in the South Caroliniana Library, Columbia. Manigault was secretary to Dr. Joseph Jones. The scrapbook contains a few Andersonville statistics for September, 1864, comments of Manigault and the press on the Wirz trial, and copies of several letters written by Andersonville prisoners. The Ohio Historical Society, Columbus, and the Library of Congress have single letters written by Andersonville inmates; another is among the Louis A. Bringier Papers, Louisiana State University, Baton Rouge. The rigid censorship under which these letters were written greatly curtails their value to the historian. Cornelia Shiver, "History of Andersonville Prison," unpublished Master's Thesis, Northwestern University, 1930, is helpful, particularly for bibliographical leads. Miss Shiver's grandparents lived within three miles of the prison.

Government Publications

The most valuable single source for information on Andersonville is *The War of the Rebellion: A Compilation of the Official Records of the Union and Confederate Armies*, 128 volumes (Washington, 1880-1901). The eight-volume second series is devoted to prisons and prisoners and volumes VI, VII, and VIII cover the Andersonville Prison period. The material consists chiefly of reports and correspondence of prison officials, consolidated returns, and reports of inspections. *The Trial of Henry Wirz*, 40th Congress, 2nd Session, House Executive Document 23 (Washington, 1868) presents the testimony of witnesses in the Wirz trial and a summary of the proceedings of the military commission conducting the case. Extreme caution is necessary in using the testimony, much of which is contradictory or absurd, but the document is helpful in reconstructing some of the details of prison management.

In 1867 the House of Representatives created a Committee on the Treatment of Prisoners of War and Union Citizens to investigate Confederate abuses of prisoners. The result was *Report of the Treatment of Prisoners of War, by the Rebel Authorities, During the War of the Rebellion: to Which Are Appended the Testimony Taken by the Committee, and Official Documents and Statistics, etc.*, 40th Congress, 3rd Session, House Report 45 (Washington, 1869). This report no doubt achieved the purpose for which it was designed, but it is of little use to one seeking factual information. The U.S. Quartermaster Department's *The Martyrs Who, for Our Country, Gave up Their Lives in the Prison Pens in Andersonville, Ga.* (Washington, 1866) is a list of names compiled from the original death register and burial list. Of more value, despite its polemical tone, is a work prepared under the direction of the surgeon general, *The Medical and Surgical History of the War of the Rebellion*, six volumes in two (Washington, 1870-83).

Connecticut, Indiana, Maine, Massachusetts, and New York have established Andersonville Monument Commissions to erect and dedicate memorials to prisoners from those states who died at Andersonville. Reports of these commissions include purblind versions of the treatment accorded inmates of the prison. The same is true of reports by the Minnesota Monument Commission, the Pennsylvania Andersonville Memorial Commission, and the Rhode Island Andersonville Monument Committee. A compilation by the Pennsylvania

Surgeon General's Office lists members of Pennsylvania regiments who died at Andersonville.

Published Diaries, Reminiscences, and Personal Narratives

Eugene Forbes, *Diary of a Soldier, and Prisoner of War in the Rebel Prisons* (Trenton, 1865) is the most useful diary by an Andersonville prisoner. Forbes's entries are longer than those of most diaries kept by Civil War soldiers, and his observations and comments are notably lacking in the bitterness that mars most later accounts. The next most helpful diary is: Donald F. Danker, editor, "Imprisoned at Andersonville: The Diary of Albert Harry Shatzel, May 5, 1864—September 12, 1864," *Nebraska History*, XXXVIII (1958), 81-125. Shatzel's grammar and spelling leave much to be desired, but his common sense and straightforwardness give his diary a rare charm. Considerably less informative but still of definite value are: E. Merton Coulter, editor, "From Spotsylvania Courthouse to Andersonville: A Diary of Darius Starr," *Georgia Historical Quarterly*, XLI (1957), 1-15; Chester McArthur Destler, editor, "A Vermonter in Andersonville: Diary of Charles Ross, 1864," *Vermont History*, XXV (1957), 229-45; "Andersonville: Diary of a Prisoner," *The Historical Magazine*, Second Series, IX (1871), 1-7; and Alfred S. Roe, *The Melvin Memorial, Sleepy Hollow Cemetery, Concord, Massachusetts; A Brother's Tribute; Exercises at Dedication, June 16, 1909* (Cambridge, 1910), in which Melvin's diary is printed (pp. 77-133). John L. Ransom, *Andersonville Diary, Escape, and List of the Dead, With Name, Co., Regiment, Date of Death, and No. of Grave in Cemetery* (Auburn, New York, 1881) has worth, but unfortunately Ransom was interested in proving that Andersonville survivors merited generous pensions and his diary obviously was amplified for publication. A ridiculous attempt to present as a diary material that is largely fiction is: Michael Dougherty, "Diary of a Civil War Hero," *Challenge*, V (1959), 9-11, 60-80.

The writer has consulted some fifty books and a dozen articles written by ex-inmates of Andersonville. Almost all of these authors wrote with the conviction that Southern leaders had conspired to liquidate Union prisoners, and at-

tribute the terrible prison conditions to deliberate Confederate
policy. For the most part their narratives are bitterly partisan,
and their value to one in search of information on what really
occurred at Andersonville depends in great measure on judi-
cious reading between the lines. The most complete account
by an ex-prisoner is: John McElroy, *Andersonville: A Story
of Rebel Military Prisons; Fifteen Months a Guest of the So-
called Southern Confederacy; A Private Soldier's Experience
in Richmond, Andersonville, Savannah, Millen, Blackshear
and Florence* (Toledo, 1879.) McElroy, a journalist, was a
better stylist than most ex-prisoner authors and his book has
enjoyed wide circulation, but it is preposterously exaggerated.
Other acrimonious narratives that have been popular are:
Robert H. Kellogg, *Life and Death in Rebel Prisons: Giving
a Complete History of the Inhuman and Barbarous Treatment of Our Brave Soldiers by Rebel Authorities, Inflicting
Terrible Suffering and Frightful Mortality, Principally at
Andersonville, Ga., and Florence, S. C., Describing Plans of
Escape, Arrival of Prisoners, with Numerous and Varied In-
cidents and Anecdotes of Prison Life* (Hartford, Connecticut,
1865); Warren Lee Goss, *The Soldier's Story of His Cap-
tivity at Andersonville, Belle Isle, and Other Rebel Prisons*
(Boston, 1868); Willard W. Glazier, *The Capture, the
Prison Pen, and the Escape; Giving a Complete History of
Prison Life in the South, Principally at Richmond, Danville,
Macon, Savannah, Charleston, Columbia, Belle Isle, Millen,
Salisbury, and Andersonville: Describing the Arrival of Pris-
oners, Plans of Escape, with Numerous and Varied Incidents
of Prison Life: Embracing, Also, the Adventures of the
Author's Escape from Columbia, South Carolina, His Re-
capture, Subsequent Escape, Recapture, Trial as Spy, and Final
Escape from Sylvania, Georgia* (New York, 1870); S. S.
Boggs, *Eighteen Months a Prisoner Under the Rebel Flag;
A Condensed Pen-Picture of Belle Isle, Danville, Andersonville, Charleston, Florence and Libby Prisons, from Actual
Experience* (Lovington, Illinois, 1887); G. E. Sabre, *Nine-
teen Months a Prisoner of War; Narrative of Lieutenant
G. E. Sabre, Second Rhode Island Cavalry, Of His Experience
in the War Prisons and Stockades of Morton, Mobile, At-
lanta, Libby, Belle Island, Andersonville, Macon, Charleston,*

and Columbia, During the Winter of 1864 and 1865 (New York, 1865) ; John W. Urban, *In Defense of the Union; Or, Through Shot and Shell and Prison Pen* (Chicago, 1887); Asa B. Isham, Henry M. Davidson, and Henry B. Furness, *Prisoners of War and Military Prisons; Personal Narratives of Experience in the Prisons at Richmond, Danville, Macon, Andersonville, Savannah, Millen, Charleston, and Columbia, With a General Account of Prison Life and Prisons in the South During the War of the Rebellion, Including Statistical Information Pertaining to Prisoners of War; Together with a List of Officers Who Were Prisoners of War from January 1, 1864* (Cincinnati, 1890) ; A. O. Abbott, *Prison Life in the South: At Richmond, Macon, Savannah, Charleston, Columbia, Charlotte, Raleigh, Goldsborough, and Andersonville, During the Years 1864 and 1865* (New York, 1865) ; and Lessel Long, *Twelve Months in Andersonville, On the March —In the Battle—In the Rebel Prison Pens, and at Last in God's Country* (Huntington, Indiana, 1896).

Three Union veterans who had been imprisoned at Andersonville wrote accounts favorable to the South. Herman A. Braun's *Andersonville: An Object Lesson on Protection* (Milwaukee, 1892) praises Wirz's management of the prison and contends that stringent control was essential to the protection —as well as the safekeeping—of the prisoners. James Madison Page's *The True Story of Andersonville Prison; A Defense of Major Henry Wirz* (New York, 1908) portrays the prison commander as a charitable humanitarian who was sorely grieved by the suffering of those in his custody. Page's attempt to defend Wirz against the wild accusations of earlier writers is marred by inaccuracies. Edward Wellington Boate, one of the Andersonville prisoners who went to Washington with the petition seeking resumption of exchange, in "The True Story of Andersonville Told by a Federal Prisoner," *Southern Historical Society Papers*, X (1882), 25-32, attributes the suffering and death at Andersonville to the impoverished condition of the Confederacy.

No reminiscence by an ex-prisoner is more venomous than the account by the judge advocate of the military commission which condemned Wirz: N. P. Chipman, *The Tragedy of Andersonville: Trial of Captain Henry Wirz, the Prison*

Keeper (San Francisco, 1911). The same year that Chipman's book was published, the sole surviving member of the commission, John Howard Stibbs, defended its work in "Andersonville and the Trial of Henry Wirz," *The Iowa Journal of History and Politics,* IX (1911). Ambrose Spencer, a Unionist who lived about nine miles from the prison and who was a prominent prosecution witness in the Wirz trial, charged the South with intentional extermination of captives in his ridiculously fallacious *A Narrative of Andersonville, Drawn from the Evidence Elicited on The Trial of Henry Wirz, the Jailer; with the Argument of Col. N. P. Chipman, Judge Advocate* (New York, 1866).

The literary output of Andersonville apologists has been much smaller than that of Northern attackers. Jefferson Davis defended Southern treatment of prisoners of war in *Andersonville and Other War Prisons* (New York, 1890). Joseph Jones's *Medical and Surgical Memoirs: Containing Investigations on the Geographical Distribution, Causes, Nature, Relations and Treatment of Various Diseases, 1855-1890* (New Orleans, 1890) gives the results of Jones's pathological investigations, and attempts to absolve the Confederacy of blame for the high mortality at Andersonville. Three officials more closely connected with the prison have wielded the pen in efforts to excuse themselves and their superiors for the tragedy. The least impassioned of these is Samuel Boyer Davis, *Escape of a Confederate Officer From Prison; What He Saw at Andersonville; How He Was Sentenced to Death and Saved by the Interposition of President Abraham Lincoln* (Norfolk, 1892). Lieutenant Davis was Wirz's second-in-command. R. Randolph Stevenson, the former "Surgeon in Charge" at Andersonville, wrote *The Southern Side, Or, Andersonville Prison* (Baltimore, 1876), which vehemently censures the Union government for "the Crime of Andersonville" and offers unconvincing arguments for its author's innocence of charges of embezzlement. An equally virulent defense of the South by a member of Wirz's staff is L. M. Park, "The 'Rebel Prison Pen' at Andersonville, Ga.," *The Southern Magazine,* (1874), 528-37.

Newspapers and Interviews

Newspapers are of little value for information on Andersonville for the simple reason that they gave very little attention to the prison. A few Andersonville items appeared in the *Augusta Daily Constitutionalist,* the *Augusta Daily Chronicle and Sentinel,* and the *Columbus Daily Enquirer.* The *New York Times* devoted more space to Andersonville than did these Southern newspapers, but the *Times* articles were based chiefly on exaggerated accounts by escaped or paroled prisoners.

Through luck and the kindness of many people, the writer located and interviewed the following descendants or kin of Confederate soldiers who were at Andersonville: Ulysses S. Lancaster, Gray, Georgia, grand-nephew of William Owens; Mrs. Ida Lee Janes, Atlanta, Georgia, daughter of Samuel Anthony Hatfield; Harold Collins, Montezuma, Georgia, son of Robert Oliver Collins; Severs James Clark, Americus, Georgia, son of Samuel Gabe Clark; Robert D. Branan, McDonough, Georgia, son of Benjamin C. Branan; and Mrs. Ivaline Dunaway, Thomaston, Georgia, granddaughter of Robert Malone Newton. Helpful information and references came from interviews with: Lonnie G. Downs, Montezuma, former mayor of Andersonville, and Mrs. J. Willis Shiver, Americus, granddaughter-in-law of Anna Hodges, whose attempt to carry vegetables to prisoners in the stockade was rebuffed.

Monographs and Miscellaneous Sources

Despite the large volume of Andersonville literature in existence, very few writers have addressed the subject in an objective spirit. The most noteworthy attempts to present dispassionate assessments of the facts are: William Best Hesseltine, *Civil War Prisons: A Study in War Psychology* (Columbus, Ohio, 1930); Rufus B. Richardson, "Andersonville," *The New Englander,* III (1880), 729-73; and Francis Trevelyan Miller, editor, *The Photographic History of the Civil War, in Ten Volumes* (New York, 1911), Vol. VII. Richard F. Hemmerlein's *Prisons and Prisoners of Civil War*

(Boston, 1934) appears at first glance to be a scholarly work, but actually it is based on limited research and marred by uncritical use of materials.

Special studies of some usefulness include: James P. Averill, *Andersonville Prison Park; Report of Its Purchase and Improvement: Accompanied by a Plat of the Grounds, Made from Actual Survey* (Atlanta, 1920); K. C. Bullard, *Over the Dead-Line, Or Who Killed "Poll Parrot"* (New York, 1909); J. W. Elarton, *Andersonville Prison and National Cemetery, Andersonville, Georgia* (Aurora, Nebraska, 1913); and Austin Flint, editor, *Contributions Relating to the Causation and Prevention of Disease, and to Camp Diseases; Together with a Report of the Diseases, etc., Among the Prisoners at Andersonville, Ga.* (New York, 1867). A recent work of fiction, MacKinlay Kantor's *Andersonville* (New York, 1955), reflects extensive research but adopts the old groundless charge that General Winder desired to kill as many prisoners as possible and portrays him working toward that end.

Index

Turncoats. *See* Traitors
Turner, J. C., 61
Turner, Maj. Thomas P., 25-27, 122
Turner, Wesley W., 4

UNITED DAUGHTERS OF THE CONFEDER-
ACY, Georgia Chapter, 121

VEGETATION, 2
Verot, Bishop Augustin, 60
Vowles, Capt. D. W., 86

WADDELL, Sgt. B. N., 61
Wallace, Gen. Lew, 16
War news, 47-48, 49
Water, 19, 26, 31, 37-38, 46-47
Whelan, Rev. Peter, 60, 71, 72, 73
White, Chief Surgeon Isaiah H., 18, 22-23, 38, 91, 94, 97-101, 103, 110, 117
White, Maj. P. W., 6, 7
Williams, Ann, 114-15
Wilson, Gen. James H., 16*n*
Winder, Brig. Gen. John H.: gets relatives appointed to prison posts, 6-7; and shortages, 8, 79-81; opposes appointment of Persons, 13; assigns Wirz to Richmond, 17; background, 27-28; reports lack of guard discipline, 56; and Raiders, 71; awareness of conditions, 75-76, 101; disciplinary measures, 76-77; and traitors, 77-78; fear of Federal raids, 82-86; conflict with Cobb, 86-88; criticism of Georgia Reserve Corps, 86-87; recommends Wirz promotion, 90; removal urged by Chandler, 90; answers Chandler, 91-95; replaces

Stevenson, 111; leaves Andersonville Prison, 113; dies, 115, 117; evaluation of, 119-20
Winder, Capt. Richard B.: constructs stockade, 4-5, 8-10; supply procurement, 5-9, 11-12, 81; transport problems, 6, 9, 11-12, 79; uncle's influence, 7; sickness of, 15; errs in cookhouse and bakery sites, 17-18; praised by Chandler, 90; accused of atrocities, 117
Winder, Capt. W. Sidney: selects prison site, 3; father's influence, 7; gets news of first prisoners, 10; relieved of command, 12; selects new prison site, 86; accused of atrocities, 117
Winder, Gen. William H., 27
Wirz, Capt. Henry (Heinrich Hartmann): background, 16-17; reports shortages, 19, 81, 94; plans sewage disposal, 19; takes disciplinary measures, 22, 51, 54, 69-72; Bowie's evaluation of, 23; Turner's report on, 25-26; unpopularity with prisoners, 43; complains of troop inefficiency, 56; and Raiders, 69-72; Chandler's praise of, 90; on Chandler report, 91-92; differs with White, 98; refuses entrance to Jones, 104; reports deaths, 110*n*; trial and execution of, 111, 117-22; commands Jeffersonville Prison, 113; notes Confederate defections, 114
Wood, 19, 32, 35-37, 47, 91. *See also* Lumber